Advanc

"Speed to market, message consistency, a
content enables will be a true competitive
impact reaches far beyond marketing, content marketing, or technical writing; it
goes straight to operational efficiencies that impact the bottom line."

Michelle Killebrew, Program Director, Digital Marketing Transformation,
IBM Cloud

"The practice and philosophy of intelligent content are critical to maximizing the
value and cost savings that content contributes to the enterprise. But intelligent
content is not the easiest concept to teach as we foster content excellence in the
organization. Consequently, we are grateful for this highly informative primer,
written by the best team imaginable for the task."

Carlos Abler, Leader, Content Marketing Strategy: Global eTransformation, 3M

"Intelligent content will become a strategic business asset powering tomorrow's
successful organizations. *Intelligent Content: A Primer* gives critical insight into the
essential shift from content hand crafting to content factory manufacturing for the
most human of activities – how we communicate. Content Industrialization is set to
revolutionize how we think about, create, edit, translate, manage, deploy, publish
and share information. Intelligent Content will transform traditional processes
through intentional design in order to create knowledge powerful enough to drive
the world's most successful companies."

Diana Ballard, Global Account Director, LOGOS GROUP

"If you've been frustrated by a content problem in your organization, open this
book now and start reading! *Intelligent Content: A Primer* tells you what happens
when you treat your content like an asset– and for most organizations, creating
intelligent content will make a real change in what's possible."

Laura Creekmore, Creek Content

"You may be new to intelligent content, but intelligent content is not new. It may
feel like disruptive technology, but it is not. It is a proven, mature methodology.
When I first encountered this methodology ten years ago, I immediately saw that it
simply makes sense. As a writer with an engineering degree, I knew it could be
applied to many types of content in many industries. This book is a primer for those
ready to learn the benefits of intelligent content. Read it and learn what is possible
with your marketing content."

Mark Lewis, Author, *DITA Metrics 101*

"When marketers start crowing that a new technique will cure all ills I'm as skeptical as the next guy, but *Intelligent Content: A Primer* really does address a number of issues at once. If your marketing goals include more efficient content teams, more personalized marketing messages, and reusable content that works across devices now and to come, intelligent content should be at the top of your to-do list."

Jenny Magic, Content Strategist, Raise Your Hand Texas

ఴఴఴఴఴఴఴఴఴఴ

"Intelligent Content provides a brilliant exposition of concepts that go against the grain of current organizational thought surrounding content, its function, and production. Reversing the outmoded view of content as a mere end-product deliverable, the authors make a strong case for recognizing content's potential as a technologically-enhanced and generative unit for creative action and enterprise. A timely book, Intelligent Content does an excellent job at mapping out the future of content production– its concepts, methods, and technologies– all of which will be of interest to forward-looking organizations aiming to competitively enhance, innovate, and future-proof their content operations."

Karl Montevirgen, Founder, Kontent Hammer

ఴఴఴఴఴఴఴఴఴఴ

"It's no secret that business is transforming and that the ability to create powerful customer experiences is at the heart of much of this evolution. Marketing doesn't change content's purpose – content changes marketing's purpose. Content is what we are. The content-driven experiences we create will define the impact we have on our consumers. If you're looking for a business reason to get intelligent about your content, this book will help you find it. These three accomplished authors deftly make the case and teach the reader about intelligent content and its place in business."

Robert Rose, Chief Strategy Officer, Content Marketing Institute

ఴఴఴఴఴఴఴఴఴఴ

"We're in the golden age of content marketing, which is wonderful. Intelligent content is no longer the side conversation, reserved for technical writers and content engineers. Intelligent content design is now part of the central conversation related to content marketing. Fortunately, we have Scott, Ann, and Charles to help us keep all that content organized. If you were looking for a starting point into working with intelligent content, this is the book you've been waiting for."

Buddy Scalera, Author, Speaker. Senior Director of Content Strategy at The Medicines Company

Intelligent Content

A Primer

Ann Rockley
Charles Cooper
Scott Abel

Intelligent Content

A Primer

Copyright © 2015 Ann Rockley, Charles Cooper, and Scott Abel

All rights reserved. No part of this book may be reproduced or transmitted in any form or by any means without the prior written permission of the copyright holder, except that brief quotations may be used with attribution, for example in a review or on social media.

Credits

Series Producer and Editor:	Scott Abel
Series Editor:	Laura Creekmore
Series Cover Designer:	Marc Posch
Publisher:	Richard Hamilton
Image Credits:	See Image Credits (p. 113)

Disclaimer

The information in this book is provided on an "as is" basis, without warranty. While every effort has been taken by the authors and XML Press in the preparation of this book, the authors and XML Press shall have neither liability nor responsibility to any person or entity with respect to any loss or damages arising from the information contained herein.

This book contains links to third-party websites that are not under the control of the authors or XML Press. The authors and XML Press are not responsible for the content of any linked site. Inclusion of a link in this book does not imply that the authors or XML Press endorse or accept any responsibility for the content of that third-party site.

Trademarks

XML Press and the XML Press logo are trademarks of XML Press.

All terms mentioned in this book that are known to be trademarks or service marks have been capitalized as appropriate. Use of a term in this book should not be regarded as affecting the validity of any trademark or service mark.

XML Press
Laguna Hills, California
http://xmlpress.net

First Edition
978-1-937434-46-5 (print)
978-1-937434-47-2 (ebook)

He who rejects change is the architect of decay. The only human institution which rejects progress is the cemetery.

—Harold Wilson, former prime minister of England

Table of Contents

Foreword

by Robert J. Glushko, UC Berkeley School of Information

Intelligent content? You might chuckle a bit when you first hear this term, because what's the alternative? Dumb content? But don't be fooled into thinking that intelligent content is just some clever new buzz phrase. Sure, the phrase is clever and pretty new, less than a decade old, but it is the perfect shorthand for talking about concepts, practices, standards, and tools for making effective use of information that have been evolving and coming together for much longer. This little book ties all of that together and is timely and easy to read, making it a good introduction – and I can't imagine a more appropriate set of co-authors.

The central idea of intelligent content is that it is adaptable to multiple purposes, document types, devices, or people. This isn't an all-or-none proposition. The amount of adaptability in formats for digital content varies on two dimensions: the degree to which the format separates semantic (what it means) information from presentation (how it looks) information and the amount of structure and organization in the semantics. A scanned print document, which is just a digital picture, is low on both of these dimensions; word processing formats are higher, especially when they use explicit formatting styles; *HTML*-encoded web pages are highly-structured but not usually semantic; and *XML* or database content is high on both dimensions, especially when it conforms to standards for describing the content types needed for different domains or activities.

Years ago I proposed the term *Information IQ* to capture this range of explicit semantics and structure in document formats (its technical qualities), but many people misunderstood and thought I was talking about digital or computer literacy. I think the term *Intelligent Content* will – and should – win out.

But no matter what we call them, the ideas that come together as intelligent content are critically important and opportune. Every system and device we interact with is getting smarter because of increased capabilities to sense, connect, and compute – and I really mean **every** system, not just smart homes and smart cars and smart phones. There is a great deal of hype about the Internet of Things, but there is also a great deal of innovation underway. If you search for the phrase "Internet of Things" along with almost any physical resource, chances are you will find something. Try "baby," "dog," "fork," "lettuce," "pajamas," "streetlamp," and you'll see what I mean. If you want to be able to design or build smart things, you need to understand the techniques and tradeoffs involved in making the intelligent content they produce and consume.

And for every system and device we explicitly interact with, there are many more invisible ones that operate and manage the physical and digital worlds we inhabit. All of them are more robust and flexible when the content they create or capture is intelligent, making it easier for machines and computers to aggregate, share, and analyze it.

Intelligent content is also easier to customize for different people and their preferred delivery channels and devices. Designers and marketers of systems and services that interact with people need to understand how contextual and transactional information can be made intelligent, making it possible to deliver higher-quality experiences by predicting unexpressed customer preferences and requests. I've called this design principle "substituting information for interaction,"[1] and it depends on having intelligent models of the information requirements for services and for the information captured and saved from previous interactions.

No one is more capable of writing about intelligent content than Ann Rockley. She began transforming mountains of printed technical documents into intelligent formats back in the 1990s,[2] when that meant *SGML*. She slowly and steadily convinced the naysayers who said, "Sounds Good, Maybe Later," that single-source publishing shouldn't be seen merely as a cost-savings tactic. Instead, she showed us that the reuse and retargetability of intelligent content were essential strategic prerequisites for businesses to succeed in an increasingly information-intensive economy characterized by rapid technology change.

I'd strongly recommend *Intelligent Content: A Primer* authored by Rockley alone, but seeing her longtime collaborator Charles Cooper here (their book, *Managing Enterprise Content: A Unified Content Strategy*[68], is a practitioner's bible) makes me even more enthusiastic. And finally, a token non-Canadian, is co-author Scott Abel, The Content Wrangler, whose marketing and evangelism through conferences and social media have brought immense new pride and professionalism to the content industries. I just can't imagine a more talented group of co-authors for this book, and I can't imagine a better place to start learning about intelligent content.

---

[1] Glushko and Nomorosa, "Substituting Information for Interaction: A Framework for Personalization in Service Encounters and Service Systems"[40]

[2] Ann Rockley, "The Impact of Single Sourcing and Technology"[65]

Preface

> Today, everything is marketing. All of the content we produce affects the customer experience. Therefore, all content is marketing and all content producers are marketers.

It used to be that we would buy a product, then look at a user manual or other post-sale content to learn how that product works. Today, however, most post-sale content is available on the Internet, and that content influences prospective buyers. Consumers may make up their minds about our products before speaking to a sales person, or they may never speak to a sales person at all.

According to Acquity, 71% of B2B customers prefer to research and buy on their own, with minimal contact with sales representatives.[1]

According to Hershey, technology buyers report that interacting with technical content is their second-most-important pre-sales activity.[2] Hershey also found that up to 70% of buying decisions are made based on "information [found] online well before a salesperson has a chance to get involved."[3]

Buyers of industrial products reported that "the only information more highly influential than pricing was detailed product information and specifications."[4]

> Content drives initial consideration.
> — McKinsey.com

There's no question that our content is more available to, and has a greater impact on, prospects and customers than at any time in the past. We need to pay attention to that impact and develop better ways of making our content serve the needs of our organizations.

---

[1] Acquity Group, "2014 State of B2B Procurement Study"[5]

[2] Michelle Blondin Hershey, "Hey, Sales & Marketing…You're not Meeting Prospects' #1 and #2 Needs!"[44]

[3] Gerhard Gschwandtner, "4 Leadership Trends in B2B Sales & Marketing"[42]

[4] Christian Bonawandt, "Your Secret Weapon to Influencing Decision Makers throughout the Buying Process"[16]

About the book

Intelligent content provides the means to take control of our content, making it easier to repurpose, more uniform in structure, and cheaper to develop. This book is a primer, an introduction to intelligent content: how it works, the benefits, the objectives, the challenges, and how to get started. Our objective is to show you why you should know about intelligent content, open the door to new ways of thinking about your content, and get you started down the road of using intelligent content to gain a competitive advantage.

This book is not a how-to book nor is it a college course or tutorial. However, we provide an extensive set of notes and references that you can use to plan your next steps.

About the audience

The audience for this book is anyone who wants to understand intelligent content, especially content marketers. It should be of equal interest to anyone who creates content and wants to improve content quality and consistency and reduce the cost of developing and maintaining content. Clients who are working with content strategists and consultants to improve their customer experience will find this book helpful in understanding the recommendations of these advisors.

Why you should read this book

For too long, the development of marketing content has been ad hoc and inefficient. In the past, marketers could tolerate those inefficiencies because the amount of pre-sales content they had to develop for customers and potential customers was relatively small.

Now, however, the amount of content available via the Internet for most products and services has exploded along with the amount of effort required to create and manage that content. Everyone who creates content that can be accessed by customers or prospects needs effective and efficient processes for developing and maintaining that content.

Intelligent content is the key to improving quality and reducing costs. We invite you to join us in exploring the possibilities that open up when you use intelligent content and the steps you can take to begin taking advantage of those possibilities.

Acknowledgments

This book would not be possible without the significant contributions of many smart, experienced, wisdom-sharing experts around the globe. We relied on specialists in engineering, technical communication, information technology, marketing, library science, communication, graphic arts, software development, translation, computational linguistics, data science, manufacturing, entertainment, content management, process engineering, law, behavioral science, mathematics, and business administration, among others. We built the strategies and approaches contained in this book on top of this multidisciplinary framework of knowledge.

Several of our peers deserve a special thank you for their help ensuring we got it right. Joe Gollner was instrumental in getting this book started, and his ideas and wisdom are evident throughout. Thanks to Robert Glushko, Rahel Anne Bailie, Mark Lewis, Padma Gillen, Laura Creekmore, Val Swisher, Diana Ballard, Sarah O'Keefe, Buddy Scalera, Scott Carothers, Karl Montevirgen, and Michelle Killebrew. To these, and many more, we owe a big thank you.

An extra special thank you is due to our amazing publisher, Richard Hamilton of XML Press. Dick spent many a night (on two coasts) working with us to ensure this book was the best it could be. His dedication and insights helped us stay on track and on time.

Ann Rockley, Charles Cooper, and Scott Abel
August, 2015

CHAPTER 1
What is Intelligent Content?

It's time to think differently about content. Instead of throwing more resources at content problems – a typical solution for many organizations – or inventing another quick fix that solves one challenge but creates more problems downstream, we need a more strategic approach.

We need a formal, repeatable, systematic way of producing content that will support us today and in the future. We need a method designed to strip away all of the productivity-zapping, unnecessary tasks that prevent us from being efficient. And, we need an approach that will allow us to focus on creating high quality content experiences at every customer touchpoint without breaking the bank.

What we need is *intelligent content*.

But, what is intelligent content? Here's the definition of intelligent content we'll use with throughout this book.[1]

> Intelligent content is designed to be modular, structured, reusable, format free, and semantically rich and, as a consequence, discoverable, reconfigurable, and adaptable.
>
> —Ann Rockley

There are two parts to this definition. The characteristics that make content intelligent (modular, structured, reusable, format-free, and semantically rich) and the capabilities we gain from adding intelligence to our content (discoverability, reconfigurability, and adaptability).

The three capabilities of intelligent content

Intelligent content is capable content. Modular, structured, reusable, format-free, and semantically rich intelligent content provides us with numerous capabilities. In this section, we'll focus on three of the most important: discoverability, reconfigurability, and adaptability.

---

[1] Definition based on Ann Rockley's article, "What is Intelligent Content?"[67], which was published in 2008.

Discoverable

Intelligent content is easily discoverable because it is enhanced with semantically rich metadata. Semantic labels help search engines deliver more relevant search results and allow computers to automatically provide content recommendations to those who may need them.

Semantic metadata also improves our ability to find and repurpose our own content, which is especially useful in organizations that produce significant amounts of content. And, semantically rich content provides translators with the context they require in order to properly localize our content – adapt it so that it's meaningful, appropriate, and effective for a particular culture, locale, or market.

Reconfigurable

Intelligent content is reconfigurable content. It is content designed to be rearranged quickly and easily, whenever customer or business needs warrant. Reconfigurable content makes it possible for us to mix-and-match content components to create new *content products* or update existing ones. Think of intelligent content components as content building blocks that can be called to duty as we see fit.

Adaptable

Intelligent content is adaptable content. It is content designed to be versatile. It's content that can be easily and automatically adjusted to meet the needs of an industry, audience segment, subject, or purpose. It can even be adapted to meet the specific needs of individual prospects and customers. And, it can be used to ensure content experiences are appropriate for the device on which our content is being consumed. Intelligent, adaptable content is required to deliver personalized content experiences.

Intelligent content makes us more capable

Modular, structured, reusable, format-free, and semantically rich intelligent content increases our capabilities. It allows us to treat content as a business asset that can help us serve customers better, increase revenue, and reduce costs. Intelligent content makes our content discoverable, reconfigurable, and adaptable, and it also equips our content with capabilities that provide additional potential benefits. We'll explore some of these in Chapter 4, *The Benefits of Intelligent Content.*

The five characteristics of intelligent content

Characteristics are qualities, attributes, or traits that distinguish one thing from another. Let's look at each of the characteristics that make content intelligent.

Modular

To be intelligent, content must be *modular*. Modular content is intentionally designed for reuse. Instead of creating documents one at a time, we create discrete components of content (modules) and assemble them into documents and other content products. Creating modular, reusable content components makes it easy to repurpose content across sets of related content – such as online help, marketing brochures, product splash pages, and product data sheets – for a product or product family.

Modular content is flexible content. We can review it and put it to use more quickly than content created using traditional approaches. We no longer need to wait until an entire content product is complete to begin review and approval. The same goes for translation. Modular content can be translated as soon as it is approved, increasing the productivity of everyone involved in the process.

Benefits of modular content include the following:

- Increased content consistency
- Improved content development agility
- Increased content production efficiency
- More opportunities for automation
- Fewer time-to-market delays

Learn more about the benefits of modular content in Chapter 4, *The Benefits of Intelligent Content*.

Structured

To be intelligent, content must be *structured*. Structured content is designed to be both human and machine readable. With structure, we can automate content delivery and manipulate content in a variety of ways. Without structure, it is almost impossible to automate content delivery.

The structure of a content component can tell a process how to display that content on different devices. For example, data that would normally be displayed as a table on a desktop computer may need alternative processing to be usable on a smartphone. However, we can only do that if we tag our content components so that processing software can determine which data need alternative processing.

Structured content is semantically-labeled and consistently organized. By providing authors with structured templates and guidelines, we can ensure that content components have a uniform structure across an organization. Consistently authored structured content gives automated processes consistent input and frees authors to think about the content itself rather than wasting time creating structure.[2]

Benefits of structured content include the following:

- Increased content consistency
- Improved content usability
- Enables guided authoring
- More opportunities for automation
- Fewer time-to-market delays

Learn more about the benefits of structured content in Chapter 4, *The Benefits of Intelligent Content*.

Reusable

To be intelligent, content must be *reusable*. Content reuse is the practice of reusing existing modular content components to develop new content products. Reusable content reduces the time required to create, manage, and publish content products and reduces translation costs significantly.

We can reuse content by manually copying it from one place and pasting it into another. Manual reuse works well until we need to update our content. Then, we have to locate all of places where we copied the content that needs to be updated. We end up relying on memory and searching, which wastes time and money and guarantees errors and omissions. With manual reuse, over time, we will end up with inconsistent content, inaccuracies, compliance problems, increased call center traffic, confused customers, and even lawsuits.

Text is the easiest type of content to design for reuse, but we can create reusable media in almost all formats. We can create modular structured content that can be either easily retrieved for manual reuse or automatically retrieved for automated reuse.

---

[2] Some technical communicators create structured content using an XML-based language such as *DocBook* or *DITA*. However, what is important is that our content be structured, not that it use any particular tool.

Benefits of reusable content include the following:

- Increased content consistency
- Reduced content production expenses
- Decreased translation cost
- More opportunities for automation
- Fewer time-to-market delays
- Reduced legal risks

Learn more about the benefits of reusable content in Chapter 4, *The Benefits of Intelligent Content.*

Format free

To be intelligent, content must be *format free*. Format-free content does not include presentation information, such as instructions about fonts, column widths, or text placement. Because intelligent content is separate from its style and formatting instructions, we can tell computers to apply the appropriate look-and-feel for the content product being created.

Format-free content lets us produce one set of content and deliver it in multiple channels (print, web, mobile) and on multiple device types (printers, desktop computers, laptops, smartphones, tablets, and other smart devices).

Benefits of format-free content include the following:

- Reduced handcrafting of content deliverables
- Improved content development agility
- Increased content production efficiency
- More opportunities for automation
- Fewer time-to-market delays

Learn more about the benefits of format-free content in Chapter 4, *The Benefits of Intelligent Content.*

Semantically rich

To be intelligent, content must be *semantically rich*. Semantically rich content is content to which we have added extra, machine-readable information that describes what the content is, what it's about, and more. We call this added information *metadata*. Computers use semantically rich metadata to understand and process content on our behalf.

Semantically rich metadata can help us locate relevant components of content needed to build customized content products for a specific industry, audience, subject, or purpose. For example, metadata can help us retrieve every occurrence of a specific type of content, such as all product descriptions, positioning statements, value propositions, setup instructions, etc.

Metadata lets us tag our content as being related to a particular industry, for example, **industry=medical** or **industry=pharmaceutical**. We might identify a content component as being targeted to a particular audience: **audience=physician, audience=pharmacist,** or **audience=patient**. Or we might use metadata to define the subject area: **subject=diabetes** or **subject=hypoglycemia** .

Benefits of semantically rich content include the following:

- Improved findability
- Reduced content production expenses
- Decreased translation cost
- More opportunities for automation
- Fewer time-to-market delays

Learn more about the benefits of semantically rich content in Chapter 4, *The Benefits of Intelligent Content.*

CHAPTER 2
Why Do We Need Intelligent Content?

Our processes are broken, we are buried in information, and it is killing our ability to satisfy our customers.

—John Mancini, President, CEO AIIM

Content. It's everywhere. It's the lifeblood of business. It's the stuff we sell. And the stuff that helps us sell. It's all the stuff that fuels business. But, creating, managing, and delivering content is a bigger challenge than it needs to be.

We live in a world in which nearly all content is processed by machines. While people create most content,[1] computers help us do just about everything else with it. And yet, despite our dependence on these increasingly useful machines, we continue to craft content in much the same way as we always have.

We use computers to create content, format it, correct it, save it, store it, find it, access it, sort it, categorize it, filter it, adapt it, enrich it, secure it, publish it, sell it, share it, curate it, deliver it, govern it, and archive it. We even rely on computers, at least in the digital world, to destroy it.

> If you can't see what's broken, it's hard to spot opportunities for improvement.

Most content production methods are based on a paper-based publishing paradigm that doesn't serve us as well today as it did in the past. Although we've made incremental changes over the last several decades – such as moving from typewriters to personal computers, adopting desktop publishing, and publishing to the web – those improvements don't address the rapid growth in the number of customer touchpoints, distribution channels, devices, and platforms, along with constantly changing customer expectations. Neither were they optimized to ensure that our content provides maximum business value.

In fact, most content improvement projects squarely aim at solving one isolated problem (fixing the website, making the app responsive, publishing to multiple channels), without much concern for whether the solution adopted will create additional challenges – and expense – in the future.

---

[1] Andrew Beaujon, "AP will use robots to write some business stories" [14]

Computers help us produce and distribute content, but we have yet to reap their biggest benefits. That's because we think of computers as assistive devices – tools that help us accomplish our jobs as we know them today. Instead, we need to harness computers as extraordinary workhorses capable of leveraging intelligent content and helping us radically reconfigure our organizations – and the way we do business – so we can achieve greatness tomorrow.

The first challenge: Lack of talent

> The most important, and indeed the truly unique, contribution of management in the 20th century was the fifty-fold increase in productivity of the manual worker in manufacturing. The most important contribution management needs to make in the 21st century is similarly to increase the productivity of knowledge work and the knowledge worker. The most valuable assets of a 20th-century company were its production equipment. The most valuable asset of a 21st-century institution, whether business or nonbusiness, will be its knowledge workers and their productivity.
>
> —Peter Drucker, *Management Challenges for the 21st Century* [29]

Over the past decade, 85% of new jobs created in the US required complex knowledge skills: analyzing content, solving problems, thinking creatively, and making informed business decisions.[2] Knowledge workers – including the people who create customer-facing content – make up over one-third of the workforce in the US, and some estimates place that percentage as high as 44%.[3]

 Despite the large number of knowledge workers, most US workplaces aren't optimized to tackle 21st century challenges. They rely on 20th century ideas grounded in outdated processes and old-school notions of work. Writers need to be concerned about more than just writing, they need to understand the technology at the intersection of computers and content.[4] Not enough writers or content strategists have this understanding.

---

[2] BizShifts-Trends, "Knowledge Workers are the Drivers of Economic Growth: They Require a Different Management Process, and Organizational Structure" [15]

[3] William G. Castellano, "Welcome to the New Normal" [18]

[4] Michael Andrews, "Should a content strategist learn to code?" [9]

And, it's not just the US that's in trouble. According to McKinsey Global Institute, by 2020, the worldwide shortage of highly skilled, college-educated knowledge workers could reach 38 million to 40 million, or 13% of demand.[56]

The second challenge: Lack of awareness

But lack of talent isn't the biggest challenge. The biggest challenge is a lack of awareness of the root problem: we need to rethink how we work.

Most executives don't understand the severity of the problem. At best, they have a clouded perception of what needs to change to meet today's content needs, never mind future content needs. In part, this is because knowledge work isn't as straightforward as product manufacturing, where tasks are relatively clear-cut and predictable, which makes processes easier to streamline and automate.

> Managers don't understand the root problem: we need to rethink how we work.

And content production processes are often not as transparent as manufacturing processes. As a result, content processes can be riddled with inefficiencies that are difficult to spot. And if you can't see what's broken, it's hard to identify opportunities for improvement. Combined with the fact that too many content creation processes aren't optimized for productivity, it's easy to see how big the challenge is.

Increasing the productivity of knowledge workers by eliminating unnecessary tasks and automating others represents a major opportunity for organizations looking to create an agile content production team that can quickly respond to opportunities and threats.

> **Note:** Process re-engineering alone won't solve the problem. Technology plays a critical role. We need software tools that will help us perform at maximum efficiency.

Some people understood this challenge early. In 2001, management guru Peter Drucker said, "Knowledge-worker productivity is the biggest of the 21st-century management challenges.... It is on their productivity, above all, that the future prosperity – and indeed the future survival – of developed economies will increasingly depend."

---

[5] Richard Dobbs, "The World at Work: Jobs, pay, and skills for 3.5 billion people" [27]

[6] Peter F. Drucker, "Knowledge-Worker Productivity: The Biggest Challenge" [28]

"Whether this advantage will translate into performance," Drucker said, "depends on the ability of the developed countries – and of every industry in them, of every company in them, of every institution in them – to raise the productivity of the knowledge worker as fast as the developed countries have raised the productivity of the manual worker in the last hundred years."[7]

The cost of an extra click, touch, or swipe

"A couple of dozen extra keystrokes per day can cost a company of one thousand workers millions of dollars (in lost productivity) per day," says David Platt, author of *Why Software Sucks and What You Can Do About It*[59]. Platt says detecting productivity bottlenecks is easy if we look critically at how we perform our jobs, step-by-step. But that's not what happens today.

Instead, Platt says, we carry on working as we have grown accustomed to working, often without noticing the barriers preventing us from achieving greatness. Eliminating all unnecessary manual tasks – and streamlining and automating the others – is needed to improve productivity, reduce errors, and leverage the time saved to innovate.[8]

Reimagining the way we work

Too much of the content we create today is handcrafted for a specific purpose and output format. As a result, we lock our content in proprietary tools and formats, making it difficult, time-consuming, and expensive to publish to multiple output channels or to create personalized content without significant rework.

With the advent of the Internet, we began the arduous process of migrating our content from the printed page to the web. That painful exercise taught us a lot. We quickly realized that our content production practices did nothing to equip us for the volume of work ahead of us. Content created for the printed page didn't work well on-screen; the screen real estate on computers was seldom consistent, the aspect ratios were different, and the resolution was terrible. And, the conversion from print to web-friendly content involved a huge amount of rework.

---

[7] Both Drucker quotes are from *Management Challenges for the 21st Century*[29]

[8] Personal communication with Scott Abel.

After years of trial-and-error, best practices emerged for writing content for the web. Lessons learned were shared. Everyone got comfortable with the new reality. But then, just when we thought we had mastered the print-to-web world, things changed again with the emergence of mobile devices (smartphones, tablets, notebooks, and other mobile computing devices). These new – and extremely popular – devices featured smaller screens and additional functionality not available elsewhere. As these devices became ubiquitous, it became evident that we were going to have to change again.

> We can't efficiently produce content for multiple formats and devices as long as our content is trapped in device-specific formats.

Responsive design helped overcome some of the challenges we face when publishing content to mobile devices, but the approach did little to help us overcome the bigger problem: the outdated way in which we create, manage, and deliver content.

What is broken, exactly? Pretty much everything. To succeed in a multi-channel, multi-screen, multi-lingual, globally connected world, we need to totally re-think our content production methods. And we need to re-imagine the value our content could provide us if it were freed from the constraints of outdated, page-centric content production methods.

What do we mean by outdated, page-centric content?

Page-centric content production techniques (word processing and desktop publishing) intermingle formatting and layout information with content. Authors create content destined for a particular output format. They decorate it (design its look and feel) for each individual output format – print, PDF, web, app, mobile, etc. The problem with this approach is that content wrapped in formatting information is difficult to reuse without significant manual intervention, which makes content unnecessarily costly to produce and time-consuming and expensive to maintain. We can't efficiently produce content for multiple formats and devices as long as our content is trapped in device-specific formats.

> In a multi-channel, multi-screen, multi-lingual, globally-connected world, we need to re-think our content production methods.

Instead of thinking about how we design content for visual appeal, we need to start thinking about what content is required, by whom, when, and in what circumstances. And we'll need to understand whether the content we create needs to work in conjunction with other content, connected computing systems, and smart devices, and if it needs to align with separate, but related, business activities.

Handcrafting deliverables does not scale. It wastes resources and doesn't improve the bottom line.

When we handcraft content for one output channel at a time, we're using an outdated approach that does not serve our business needs today. Handcrafting deliverables does not scale. Compared to intelligent content, it wastes time, money, and talent and provides limited business value.

On the other hand, intelligent content is intentionally designed for reuse and repurposing, optimized for efficiency, and created and managed using a scaleable, future-proof approach. Intelligent content is content for today – and the future.

Dramatically transforming the way we create, manage, and deliver content using a new approach can be disruptive, especially when new skills, roles, responsibilities, and tools are added to the equation. But, once we understand how intelligent content works and why we need it, we will recognize why we cannot continue to work as we have in the past. We need new ways of working to succeed.

Our future content must be intelligent.

CHAPTER 3
Why Do Content Marketers Need Intelligent Content?

Content marketers are tasked with creating and distributing valuable, relevant, and consistent content to attract and retain a clearly-defined audience and, ultimately, to drive profitable customer action.[1] To do so effectively, they must deliver the right content to the right prospect at the right time – content designed to serve the needs of existing customers or to convert prospects into new customers. In today's multi-channel world, content must be designed to support a constantly changing landscape of devices, platforms, and channels, making content marketing production increasingly challenging – and expensive.

Just how expensive?

Research conducted in 2015 by Gleanster Research found that B2B content marketers in the US spend over two-thirds of their time – and an estimated $5.2B annually – producing content.[2] Despite the large commitment in time and money, B2B content marketers say their biggest challenges include their inability to meet deadlines (92%), redundant content creation efforts (90%), difficulties coordinating content creators (81%), and challenges repurposing content (64%). Mid-to-large sized B2B firms waste twenty-five cents of every dollar spent on content marketing production because of inefficient methods.[3]

Gleanster found that organizations that invest in streamlining and optimizing content marketing production produce two times more content than their less efficient competitors, and they do so 163% faster.[3] And size plays a role in inefficiency. The bigger the

> Twenty-five cents of every dollar spent on content marketing production is wasted.

organization, the more likely they are to waste time and money performing unnecessary and redundant tasks.

---

[1] Content Marketing Institute, "What is Content Marketing?"[23]

[2] Gleanster Research, "The $958M Marketing Problem"[36]

[3] Ian Michiels,"Measuring Inefficiency in Your Content Marketing Production Processes"[52]

However, productivity issues and meeting deadlines aren't the only challenges facing content marketers.

Ask any marketer what a great marketing campaign looks like, and you might be surprised just how uninspiring the answer is. According to the Direct Marketing Association, the average successful direct marketing campaign (snail mail) has around a 4.4% conversion rate (10 to 30 times better than email). Very successful campaigns might reach 6%.[4]

> Six percent? Seriously? In what other industry would 94% failure get you an opportunity to do a case study presentation on your success? Only in marketing. That's got to change.

Marketers need to move past the spray-and-pray marketing techniques that have dominated their discipline for decades.[5] Creating personas and aiming content at members of imaginary groups is no longer enough. Today, marketers need to do better. They need to marry information about the individuals they hope to convert with information development management techniques designed to deliver the right pieces of content to those individuals at the right time on the devices of their choosing.[6]

One final challenge facing content marketers is determining how to use content to provide an exceptional experience for two different, but related groups: prospects and existing customers.

According to research from Gartner, more than 90% of organizations don't have a formal content strategy in place to ensure the content they produce is consistent across all customer touch points.[7] Consequently, the customer journey is riddled with inconsistent, frustrating, and confusing experiences that leave customers wondering, "What happened?"

Once a prospect buys a product or service and becomes our customer, problems begin. Content is no longer familiar, and the instructions don't look, feel, or sound anything like the marketing and sales materials. Neither does the service contract, the warranty, the customer support website, the product documentation, or the training materials. For no good reason, the content experience changes drastically – and not in a

---

[4] Allison Schiff, "Direct Mail Response Rates Beat Digital"[71]

[5] "Are You Guilty of Using a 'Spray & Pray Marketing' Approach to Attract Your Target Market?"[58]

[6] Glenn Taylor, "B2B Content Preferences Survey: Buyers Want Short, Visual, Mobile-Optimized Content"[78]

[7] "Gartner Says Less than 10% of Enterprises Have a True Information Strategy"[35]

good way. That's why organizations that recognize the importance of a unified customer experience have started rethinking what it means to be customer-centric.

But, most organizations aren't organized around the customer. Instead, they're organized as companies always have been – around the corporate hierarchy, each department nestled comfortably into a walled garden. Protected. Separate. Different. Silo-ed. Cut off from the people who produce content in other departments.

A company organized in silos cannot produce a unified customer experience. Silos ensure content inconsistency and make it impossible for an organization to speak with one voice. That's because marketers working in isolation from customer support have no idea why customers call the help hotline. The training department creates content without any involvement from the documentation team. And the technical support staff has no idea what the folks in sales are telling prospects.

But, when companies recognize that the content they create – regardless of who created it or for what purposes – has a direct impact on customer experience, silos come down. They start thinking strategically and discard old models. Collaboration becomes the norm. Customers notice.

What kind of content?

There's a big disconnect between the content we produce and the content that prospects and customers want and need. To provide value, we need to rethink our content and who should be involved in its production.

We need to provide appealing content to the audience we hope to attract and engage. We need content that gives prospects and existing customers a consistent experience with our brand, regardless of which department creates that content.[8]

And we must adjust to the new reality: Content that we previously viewed as post-sale (how-to videos, product documentation, and training materials) influences buying decisions.[9] Savvy brands are breaking down silos between departments. Sales, marketing, PR, technical documentation, support, and training no longer operate in isolation from one another. Everyone who creates content works together.

---

[8] Scott Abel, "Lip Service is No Longer Enough: Why You Need a Unified Customer Experience Strategy"[3]

[9] John Rugh, "Earn a Customer for Life with Post-Sale Content Marketing"[69]

 There's momentum toward the adoption of intelligent content in the content marketing field. In 2014, Content Marketing Institute (CMI) bought the Intelligent Content Conference from The Rockley Group.[10] CMI did so because they understand that content marketing must mature in order to thrive. And they know that without guidance, it's likely that marketers will make the same unnecessary and avoidable mistakes that other content professionals have made before.

These are just some of the reasons content marketers need intelligent content.

---

[10] "Content Marketing Institute Acquires Intelligent Content Conference (ICC)"[2]

CHAPTER 4
The Benefits of Intelligent Content

Intelligent content contributes to the bottom line. Let's take a look at some of the most common ways intelligent content can make us more profitable. The first benefit is an easy sell: we write content once and reuse it many times. Instead of creating documents, we create discrete content components, which can be assembled into documents, pushed into apps, or served up dynamically on the web. Because they are intentionally designed for reuse, we can repurpose content components – often automatically – in slide decks, white papers, reports, infographics, or on social networks. And we can mix and match components in a variety of combinations. The possibilities are almost endless.

But content reuse is not the only benefit. If we're creating content for use across multiple formats (paper, web, apps), or if our content will be consumed on more than one device type (tablets, smartphones, laptops, notebooks, desktop computers), adopting intelligent content will make us far more efficient, improving our bottom line.

Rather than focusing our efforts on producing content for a single channel or format, we can use intelligent content to efficiently adapt our content for display wherever we need it. When a new device type emerges – even one that no one expected – our content will be positioned to take advantage of the capabilities of that device, with minimal time and effort.

> Intelligent content makes us far more efficient, improving our bottom line.

While intelligent content comes with up-front costs, once fully implemented, it reduces *document* creation, editing, and review time, improving productivity and saving costs.

If we translate, localize, or personalize our content, adopting intelligent content can provide dramatic cost savings over traditional content production methods.[1] In fact, in many multi-lingual environments, we can recover the cost of adopting intelligent content within a matter of months through savings in translation alone.

---

[1] Amber Swope, "Calculating the Financial Impact of DITA for Translation"[77]

In addition, intelligent content can help us enhance the customer experience by improving the quality of our content – its accuracy, accessibility, and usability – and making it easier for prospects and customers to find the content they need.

All in all, intelligent content provides significant advantages over creating content in the traditional manner.

Contributing to the bottom line

Intelligent content contributes to the bottom line in many ways.

Increased sales

Many organizations struggle to create and deliver fresh, relevant content for prospects and customers, which leads to lost sales opportunities.[2] This happens because traditional content production methods were not designed for an always-on, multi-channel, multi-platform world.

Consumers today expect brands to deliver an exceptional content experience every time – the right content, at the right time, in the right language, in the right format, and on the right device. That's bad news for organizations challenged with content product inefficiencies. Content drives sales. If we can't produce the content our prospects and customers are looking for, we lose the opportunity to serve them. The inability to efficiently produce content is especially troublesome because consumers today are actively seeking content about products and services before they connect with the brand. Survey data indicates that among B2B consumers, somewhere between 60–70% of the buying decision is based solely on content found online.[3]

Content production inefficiencies aren't the only problem preventing us from increasing sales with content. So, too, is our inability to create personalized content. Intelligent content provides us with a level of control not available from traditional content production approaches. Being able to provide personalized, highly relevant content experiences can help us meet changing consumer expectations.[4]

---

[2] Feldman and Sherman, "The High Cost of Not Finding Information"[34]

[3] Gerhard Gschwandtner, "Four Leadership Trends in B2B Sales and Marketing"[42] and CEB, "Sell How Your Customers Want to Buy"[19]

[4] Adobe Systems, "The Personalization Payoff: The ROI of Getting Personal"[7]

How do we know consumers value personalized content? First, consumer surveys consistently show a preference toward greater personalization.[5] Second, companies that consistently leverage personalized content report increased sales.

Personalized calls to action[6] and personalized product recommendations[7] outperform generic content. In fact, according to sales data from over 250 million shoppers, customer-focused content delivers a 25% increase in online sales and a 300% improvement in customer lifetime value.[8]

And that's not all, personalized content experiences that take advantage of location help increase sales further. 62% of adults under 34 are willing to share their location with brands in exchange for more relevant content.[6] Auto-seller Edmunds.com reported an 18% increase in conversion when they gave repeat customers content that took into consideration their location and their preferred channel for consuming content.[9]

To earn new business from prospects and maintain the loyalty of existing clients, we must provide appropriate content quickly. Intelligent content can help us rapidly create and deliver personalized content experiences.

For an example of leveraging intelligent content to unlock value from content, see Chapter 7, *Opportunity: Increasing Service Revenue*.

Increased productivity

Inefficient content production prevents us from beating the competition. Consider The New York Times. In 2014, an internal evaluation ("The New York Times Innovation Report"[55]) was leaked to the press. The 97-page report revealed that the company culture and its ideas about publishing were woefully out-of-date. One of the most notable challenges mentioned in the report was the paper's inability to reuse legacy content to create new content products.

New York Times senior product manager Andrew Phelps (co-author of "The New York Times Innovation Report") decided to try an experiment.

---

[5] CMO by Adobe, "Retailers Seek Innovation In Personalization"[22] and Karen Freeman, et al., "Three Myths about What Customers Want"[43]

[6] Anum Hussain, "Personalized Calls-to-Action Convert 42% Better"[46]

[7] Elyse Dupre, "80% of Americans Enjoy Purchase-Based Recommendations in Email"[30]

[8] MyBuys.com, "MyBuys / etailing group Consumer Survey Reveals Customer-Centric Marketing Drives Buyer Readiness and Purchases"[54]

[9] Courtney Eckerle, "Offer Relevance: How Edmunds.com achieved an 18% increase in price quote requests through personalized targeted marketing"[31]

He manually assembled a collection of legacy content (obituaries from 2014) into a new product The Times called a *collection*.[10] That product was repackaged and published on Flipboard, a visual news aggregator and mobile app. That collection became the most popular collection of content in the history of Flipboard and was responsible for driving traffic back to the Times website.

The Times report pointed out the value of reusing previously vetted and published legacy content to assemble collections, but noted that manual reuse was slow, cumbersome, error-prone, and not scalable. Because their content was not intelligent — it was unstructured and the tools they used to produce content were designed around a print publishing paradigm — the paper was unable to create collections as fast as their more nimble digital publishing competitors.

"We have a tendency to pour resources into big one-time projects, work through the one-time fixes needed to create them, then overlook the less glamorous work of creating tools, templates and permanent fixes that cumulatively can have a bigger impact by saving our digital journalists time and elevating the whole report," the report authors wrote. "We greatly undervalue replicability."

Most organizations today face similar productivity challenges, which remain largely unnoticed by executive leadership. For example, management may be unaware that knowledge workers responsible for creating content spend 36% of their work day looking for — and manually reusing — content spread across an array of systems in a mixture of formats. And, 56% of the time, they can't find the content needed to complete the job. When they're unable to locate the content they need, they recreate it, further wasting limited corporate resources.[11]

Not finding the right content comes at significant cost. Bad (and potentially costly) business decisions are likely to be made based on incorrect or inconsistent content. Productivity is damaged when content is unknowingly recreated in other parts of the organization. Sales opportunities are damaged when salespeople cannot find the content they need or end up spending significant time reworking the content they do find to make it work for their purposes.

---

[10] New York Times, "Notable Deaths 2014"[56]

[11] Feldman and Sherman, "The High Cost of Not Finding Information"[34]

Intelligent content makes us more efficient. It eliminates rework. It provides us with capabilities that can help us overcome obstacles, eliminate weaknesses, and defend against competitive forces aiming to disrupt business as usual.

Intelligent content removes the bottlenecks that slow down traditional content production approaches, streamlining the entire process. Implemented correctly, intelligent content can help turn our firms into hyper-efficient content producing factories.

Agile content

Agile development processes are being adopted in nearly every industry around the globe.[12] A recent survey found the number of teams in the technology sector that use agile processes has doubled, rising from 35% in 2013 to 76% in 2014.[13] While software developers and IT departments make up the majority of agile practitioners, HR, marketing, sales, technical communication, support, and training departments are also using the approach.

Agile processes emphasize rapid iteration and incremental change. Our content also needs to be agile so we can respond quickly to competitive threats, changing customer needs, regulatory requirements, and innovations in technology.

As content strategy guru Rahel Anne Bailie points out, the agility intelligent content provides allows us to "reclaim the time – and money – otherwise wasted on searching for, editing, copy-and-pasting, re-editing, formatting, fixing, testing, and otherwise manipulating content" and use those resources to innovate.

Intelligent content is agile because it is modular. We don't need to wait until an entire document, portion of a website, or set of information is complete to review and translate it; we can produce content module by module. This makes content available to those who need it much sooner than in traditional publishing paradigms.

Reduced translation cost

Organizations that create content in multiple languages can enjoy significant reductions in translation expense by adopting intelligent content.

---

[12] Veracode.com, "Companies Worldwide Are Adopting Agile Development Techniques"[79]

[13] Versionone.com, "8th Annual State of Agile Survey"[80]

That's because intelligent content allows us to translate content components once and automatically reuse those translations in multiple content products, extending the *return on investment* from content reuse across our multilingual content.[14] Just as we intentionally reuse content components produced in our source language, we can similarly reuse translated content produced in our target languages. [15]

But the savings don't stop there. Intelligent content is controlled content. Because we know which content components we have updated in our source language, we can control the number of words sent to translation. Instead of sending an entire content product to be translated, intelligent content allows us to send only the components of content that need to be translated – new content and content that has changed since the last translation. And there's no need to wait until the final deliverables are ready for review. We can send translated content components for review and approval as they become available, reducing delays.

Reusing translated intelligent content also slashes two time-consuming and expensive hidden costs: in-country review and desktop publishing.

To ensure our content resonates with target audiences in other markets, we often arrange for it to be reviewed – and localized – by someone in the region. Referred to as in-country reviews, the adaptations made to content during this phase are designed to make our content more meaningful, appropriate, and effective. It's more than translation. And, depending on the complexity of the content and the intent of our communication, in-country review iterations can be very expensive in terms of time and money. The fewer reviews, the more we save – and the faster our content is ready for publishing.

Finally, by separating translated content from formatting information – creating format-free content – we can save significant money on desktop publishing (DTP).[16] How much money? In some organizations, fees paid to translation firms for DTP services can exceed the cost of translating the words. By using language-specific templates that account for differences in content such as text expansion and right-to-left lan-

---

[14] Sarah O'Keefe, "Calculating the ROI of DITA"[72]

[15] Ann Rockley, "Best Practices: Creating a Winning ROI"[66]

[16] Val Swisher, "Intelligent Content Meets Translation"[76]

guages, DTP costs are minimized.[17] And by automating publication, we can eliminate the traditional copy/paste and layout steps, significantly reducing DTP costs and eliminating errors.

Reduced risk

Content must be current and accurate wherever it appears. Errors, omissions, inconsistencies and inaccuracies can introduce unnecessary and expensive risks. Problems with content can damage brand, taint reputation, and cause us to run afoul of rules, regulations, and laws. They can even cause death.

Most content problems that increase risk are due to a lack of control. Consider this embarrassing – and expensive – 2006 content snafu intentionally created by an employee of Manchester, UK, luncheon meat manufacturer, H. R. Hargreaves & Son.[18]

> A British meat processor on Tuesday was frantically trying to recall packages of sliced ham that list dog excrement as one of the ingredients.
>
> Mick Woods, 34, told The Mirror he lost his appetite when he opened the $1.75 package labeled as "premium," and read the ingredients. Among them was a listing of "Dog Sh--," he told the newspaper.
>
> He said he and wife laughed long and hard, but didn't eat any of the ham.
>
> Meanwhile, officials with Manchester meat manufacturer H.R. Hargreaves & Son were scrambling to get all of the affected packages recalled from stores before they could make it into consumers' homes.
>
> The labeling prank was pulled by an employee who has since been fired, the report said.
> —Source: United Press International, January 31, 2006

Intentionally introduced errors are both disconcerting and potentially expensive. In the case of Hargreaves Ham, the manufacturer failed to control the content of their product label, leading to a troublesome (albeit humorous) public relations issue and unnecessary expenses associated with product recall. When a company fails to control content and those

---

[17] The Content Wrangler, "L10N Reality Check: Industry Insider Shines Light on the Dirty Little Secrets of the Translation and Localization Industry that You Won't Learn at a Webinar"[10]

[18] Jan Disley, "Exclusive: Poo Listed on Ham Ingredients"[26]

who create it, the fallout can damage brand, potentially resulting in lower sales, litigation, and injury.

It's not only intentionally introduced content problems that are problematic. In regulated environments, content control is absolutely critical; every claim must be substantiated. Claims made are scrutinized by regulators who look for — and penalize companies for — inconsistencies. Penalties may involve warnings or fines, and, in situations where errors and inconsistencies could cause injury or death (think pharmaceutical and medical device manufacturers), regulators can shut a factory down. As was the case with Hargreaves, media attention introduces additional challenges.

We can reduce the risk of inaccurate and incorrect information when we use intelligent content. Because intelligent content is controlled content, we can quickly discover and correct errors and omissions before they wreak havoc.

CHAPTER 5
Intelligent Content in the Organization

You will find opportunities to apply intelligent content in many places in your organization. This chapter discusses some of the types of information that can benefit from intelligent content.

Content marketing information

> Content marketing is a strategic marketing approach focused on creating and distributing valuable, relevant, and consistent content to attract and acquire a clearly defined audience and, ultimately, to drive profitable customer action.
> —Content Marketing Institute, *What is Content Marketing?*[23]

Content marketing doesn't attempt to directly sell a product or service. If we are trying to engage prospects or customers, we need to create content that reaches them on an ongoing basis, not just occasionally. Creating increasing amounts of content can be daunting, especially with limited resources. This is where intelligent content plays a key role.

Joe Pulizzi, the father of content marketing and author of the book *Epic Content Marketing*[61], talks about the 10-to-1 rule: don't just create one piece of content; create 10 pieces of content from the same material. Build your content to create a whole suite of materials.

For example, with proper planning we can use intelligent content to create a series of blog posts and compile them into a white paper. Or we could create a series of white papers and compile them into an eBook or create a white paper and publish stand-alone portions as a series of blog posts. We could take key points from the blog and post them to Facebook, LinkedIn, or Twitter. We could create a video testimonial or story and transcribe the video to create a blog. We could create short and long versions of a story, post the short version on Facebook, and point readers to the full story.

With intelligent content, we can turn one deliverable into 5, 10, or more. And, when we add languages to the mix, intelligent content can help us become a global content marketing powerhouse.

Traditional marketing content

Traditional marketing content often has a tremendous amount of reuse potential. We can reuse value propositions, feature and benefit statements, product or service descriptions, and calls to action across many different marketing assets.

We can design marketing content to be reused, repurposed, and automatically published to web and mobile devices, and we can even repurpose such content into print formats such as brochures or print ads.

Product and support content

This kind of informational content supports customers once they have bought a product or service.

Often a company sells variations of a product or similar products in a product family. With intelligent content, we can reuse common content components across product lines and across different types of content products. For example, we could reuse product and service content in training materials, augmented with exercises and activities.

Many customers don't want static, generic content aimed at the masses. They want personalized, *dynamic content* intentionally designed to serve their needs. With intelligent content we can use a customer profile to automatically display only the content that is relevant to that customer. And that content can be adapted based on the customer's role (e.g., influencer vs. decision maker), region, product, language, or any other characteristic.

If we have a product or service that can be configured by customers, intelligent content can be designed to serve their specific needs. Intelligent content can automatically adapt itself to provide content that is relevant to an individual customer, based on the configuration that customer purchased. The alternative would be to pre-document all of the potential iterations of a configurable product, which is impractical, if not impossible. With intelligent content, business rules, and powerful retrieval tools, content can be automatically adapted to the needs of individual customers.

Figure 5.1 shows how we might build a customer guide and a technician page by reusing intelligent content from a CMS.

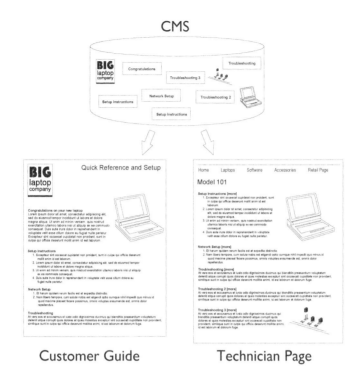

Figure 5.1 – Customer and technician page from CMS

Learning and training content

Learning plays a critical role in every organization. A highly trained workforce is productive and effective; it can adapt quickly to changes in the market and to customer requirements. In this section, we look at several common training approaches and examine the benefits intelligent content can provide.

Instructor-led training, either in person or virtually, typically uses a combination of slide decks and supplementary materials. Both in-person instructor-led and virtual instructor-led classroom training require us to prepare customized content for both instructors and students. Intelligent content allows us to create all the materials needed from a single source of content. And, we can customize them for the audience. We can use conditional content and automated publishing to ensure both students and instructors are provided with the right content.

eLearning provides web-based training for self-paced learners. eLearning materials often reuse content from instructor-led or virtual training courses, but in a more interactive, media-rich environment. Traditionally, simulations, videos, and other interactive materials tend to be created as a single chunk of content, making it difficult to swap languages, images, or change interactive content, without reworking the  materials. But, intelligent content changes all of that. Like text, simulations, animations, and video tutorials can be modularized. When we need localized content, we can use conditional content to serve the right components of audio narration – in the right language – automatically.

Learning has moved from the classroom to the desktop and, recently, to mobile. With smartphones, tablets, laptops, and other connected devices, learners can attend class wherever they are. Mobile learning (also called mLearning) delivers material in bite-sized pieces whenever students have time. Intelligent content enables mLearning content to be delivered on-demand, anywhere, any time, and on any device.

Employee-focused content

Content provided to employees by employers is known as employee-focused content. It's information we need to know about the way we work, including policies, procedures, benefits, employment, safety, working hours, holidays, sick leave, and more. Employee-focused content can vary by role (e.g., based on job title) or by some other condition (e.g., length of employment).

Traditionally, employee-based content was published in employee handbooks, in job aids, or to the corporate intranet. It was treated as one big content product (here's everything you need to know to work here), or it was published piecemeal in a patchwork of content (if you look in enough places, perhaps you'll find what you need). In both situations, employees had to search for content that applied to them. Far too often, they failed to find what they were looking for and either stopped looking or asked co-workers, with predictably unreliable results.

Today organizations are turning to dynamic intelligent content to help them deliver the right piece of content to the right employee, configured specifically to meet their needs. Intelligent content can help us provide relevant information on-demand, in a fraction of the time it would take employees to search for and find content on their own.

CHAPTER 6
Opportunity: Increasing Customer Engagement

The term engagement can be defined in several ways:

1. an agreement to do something;
2. a period of employment (especially for a performer);
3. a hostile encounter between armies;
4. an emotional involvement or commitment.

The last definition is what we're looking for.

We want customers to be engaged with the content we provide. Admittedly, the engagement may be fleeting – telling the customer how to complete a task or answering a question about our products or services. But it may last longer and require a deeper commitment from both sides. That longer, more committed relationship might be a months-long advertising campaign. Or it might be more personal, such as the interaction a patient would have with the content displayed on a medical device.

Either way, we want readers to pay attention and be engaged when they experience our content. Of course, we want to create great content, but what makes content great is subjective and depends on the needs of the user at the time.

Some content must be concise – short and to the point. Emergency information usually falls into this category. We don't need to know the biography of English physician and circulatory system expert William Harvey when we're trying to stop a wound from bleeding! If we want to tell our reader something, help solve a problem, or sell a product, service, or process, we may need only a short, easy-to-read component of information. If it meets that reader's needs at the time, then it's great content.

On the other hand, not all content should be transactional. We may want develop a longer-term relationship with a prospective customer, one where we provide information or build a rapport. We may want to educate or create interest in our product, service, or process, but we don't expect that to happen with a single click or a single reading. Instead, we want to build interest over the long-term with the hope that when prospective customers are ready to decide, they will come back to us.

How can we do that?

The best way is to provide readers with the information they want, where and when they want it. This means we need to provide both concise bits of transactional content as well as longer, more engaging content designed to convert a sales prospect into a customer, help an employee navigate a complicated transaction, or move an existing customer toward the purchase of an upgrade.

Intelligent content can help us with both. That's because intelligent content focuses on creating discrete, modular, and reusable content components that can be combined to meet the needs of our readers.

Of course, content shouldn't be defined or tagged just by its length; we can also define and tag it by its purpose. We might identify content that provides background information, helps readers complete a task, or serves an immediate information need. Or we can tag content to make it easier to personalize it to meet readers' preferences, such as language or screen size. Other, less obvious, criteria include location, device orientation, connection speed, and customer mood.

Content creators can find it difficult to determine the right amount of information to deliver in each situation. We want readers to have what they need, but we don't want to overwhelm.

Here are two time-tested methods that can help us give readers related content when they want it without overwhelming them.

Linking

The first method is to provide links to information that is closely related to the content being viewed. It may be background information, similar information, or information that leads readers on a path of discovery. The key is that readers get to choose their own path through our content.

We've all seen this type of information before, probably without realizing it. Amazon calls it "Customers Who Bought This Item Also Bought." On eBay, it's next to the title "Related." Etsy calls it "Related to," and Kickstarter suggests "You might also like." Whatever they're called, such links offer readers information related to what they're currently looking at or have recently viewed.

Progressive disclosure

The theory behind progressive disclosure is similar to linking, but the two methods differ in practice. Both methods provide additional inform-ation that the customer might need, but progressive disclosure reveals information as the customer requires it, rather than simply listing related information in one place all at once.

Progressive disclosure lets readers concentrate on the task at hand, and doesn't force them to filter out information noise they may not need at the time.[1] As readers progress, we automatically serve the next piece of relevant information as they need it.

Figure 6.1 shows a page for a technician that uses progressive disclosure. The page contains sections with setup and troubleshooting information. Each section has a **[more]** button that, when clicked, reveals additional information about that topic. Readers can move through the content sequentially and select which areas they want to examine more closely.

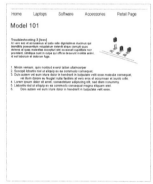

Technician Page   Progressive Disclosure

Figure 6.1 – Progressive disclosure

Intelligent content supports both methods. The structure and tagging in intelligent content allow us to publish content on an as-required basis for progressive disclosure or to create links to related information.

---

[1] Jakob Nielsen, "Progressive Disclosure"[57]

CHAPTER 7
Opportunity: Increasing Service Revenue

On average, service organizations are three times as profitable as their related business units. Although service revenue represents just over 25% of total revenue, it delivers 46% of the profits.[1]

Specialized equipment makers, for example, medical imaging manufacturers, rely on revenue from service visits (inspection, maintenance, and repair). The more service visits, the more profit. To maximize profitability, savvy manufacturers optimize field service visits and the work associated with them.

A forward-thinking manufacturer might adopt intelligent content to help squeeze an extra appointment into each day, providing additional revenue for the company without increasing labor costs.

Leveraging intelligent content, a company can create a hyper-efficient service organization that produces additional revenue by stripping away the unnecessary tasks and fine-tuning the remainder.

By connecting semantically rich, structured content (things like product maintenance and repair instructions) to existing databases of information (things like appointment calendars, maps and directions, equipment inventories, customer relationship management systems, and invoicing) the organization can leverage the power of intelligent content to drastically speed up the entire process.

Let's look at a possible scenario that leverages intelligent content to streamline service visits for a company that manufactures medical imaging equipment.

[1] Jeffrey Glueck et al., "The Service Revolution: Manufacturing's Missing Crown Jewel" [38]

The scenario:

A technician – we'll call him Pete – arrives at his first appointment. Guided there with the help of an integrated appointment calendar (so he's on time) and driving instructions (to make certain he's at the right place), Pete parks, enters the facility, and locates the equipment that needs service. He takes out his iPad, launches a diagnostics application, takes a photo of the equipment, and in a few seconds, a detailed, 3D representation of the machine he's standing in front of appears on screen.

He inspects the imaging equipment and determines the likely cause of the malfunction (a short circuit). On his iPad, he opens the repair instructions. He scans the *QR code* on the part he believes needs to be replaced, and the repair instructions for that part appear on the screen next to an image.

Savvy manufacturers optimize field service visits to maximize revenue.

Before Pete begins the repair, the instructions (intelligent content) trigger an on-screen message asking if he would like to confirm whether the needed parts and tools are available in his truck, which is parked in a garage a few blocks away. He agrees, and a query is sent to a database that tracks the inventory of parts and tools on each repair truck. Once the needed parts and tools are verified as being on his truck, Pete can, with customer approval, begin the repair.

First, however, the repair instructions again trigger an on-screen message. This time the message asks if Pete would like to start an estimate for the proposed work. He agrees. With a few taps, he temporarily removes the parts and tools from the truck inventory and creates an estimate for the client to review. Customer information for the estimate is drawn from the customer database at headquarters.

Pete finds the customer, presents the estimate, and seeks approval of the repair work. The customer agrees and signs the estimate (on the iPad screen), which is automatically converted to an invoice that will be sent to the customer once the job is completed. The parts and tools used in the repair are automatically removed from the truck inventory, which triggers the system to send a message to the inventory control department to restock the truck when it returns to the warehouse.

Intelligent content can help service organizations streamline their entire field service business, driving the kind of hyper-efficient process described in our scenario. But the possibilities are much broader.

Intelligent content drives process improvements such as more accurately forecasting sales and profits, guaranteeing the availability of parts and tools, optimizing field service visits, kick-starting related business processes, reducing bottlenecks, maximizing productivity, and much more.[2]

Without intelligent content, service organizations will likely drown under the weight of their own unintelligent content, unable to keep up with more agile, disruptive, and future-looking competition.

A vision of the future

A key objective for senior executives over the next several years is to use disruptive technology to get closer to customers to improve relationships, and enhance experiences. This is a critical path where businesses must not only commit to new technology and goals, but also invest in the methodologies, systems, processes, and people to bring about change from within before it can effectively engage outside.
—Brian Solis, "A Critical Path for Customer Relevance, Part 1"[74]

Imagine a future world in which content is equipped with superpowers. A world in which content isn't just something we passively consume but, instead, is something that we rely upon to work on our behalf. A world in which computers use content to drive automated tasks, trigger business processes, optimize production schedules, reduce costs, eliminate errors, spot risks, prevent disasters, and totally streamline the world of modern business. A world in which content enables us to do better work – and more of it – with fewer resources. A world in which content is center stage, the main character in the play, empowered, with the help of computers, to transform traditional companies into innovative, hyper-efficient, content-centric organizations.

Today, all of these things – and more – are possible. There's no need to imagine a future world in which content can provide you with staggering business value. Intelligent content currently can – and does – help savvy organizations optimize and streamline operations.

---

[2] Glushko and McGrath, *Document Engineering*[39]

CHAPTER 8
Opportunity: Preparing Content for the Future

What does it mean to prepare your content for the future? And, why would we want to do that, anyway?

Publishing is a living discipline with one constant: change. Folks who have been in business – any business – for more than a few years, know what we're talking about. But for those who are new to the space, or aren't old enough to have lived through the past three decades of content production approaches, here's a summary.

In the 1980s, we relied on paper, typewriters, Letraset® rub-on lettering,[1] and waxers[2] to create and paste up[3] content. Then desktop publishing systems[4] and personal computers replaced all of that (except paper, of course).

Then, we started to put our content on the web. In the early days, things were pretty simple – our customer was probably using a dial-up modem, and their screens could display 640x480 pixels in a whopping 256 colors. It didn't matter what our content was – a technical manual or a full-color ad (remember banner ads?) – we had limited scope for creative expression.

We hard-coded image sizes into HTML pages and embedded fonts into paragraphs because that's how things were done. But when computer monitors got larger and could display more colors and we packed up and put away our dial-up modems, our content was still stuck in the past. To display content effectively, we had to go back and strip out all that hard-coded formatting. That content was not future-proofed.

Today, we expect to be able to access the information we need wherever we are. We're not tied to desks, large monitors, power cords, or Ethernet

---

[1] https://en.wikipedia.org/wiki/Letraset

[2] Purplefusion, "Remembering a classic: The Wax Machine"[62]

[3] https://en.wikipedia.org/wiki/Paste_up

[4] https://en.wikipedia.org/wiki/Desktop_publishing

cables. The equipment that once took up a full workstation (and more) now fits in our pocket. A camera, video recorder and player, typewriter, audio player, calculator, notepad, dictionary, etc., now all fit into a small, thin package – the modern smartphone.

Because smartphones are ubiquitous,[5] many people make the incorrect assumption that we should focus our efforts on designing content for small screens. Bad idea.

Many corporate boardrooms have replaced data projectors with large (>50 inch) display units. And it's not just businesses that have large screens. Home theaters with similar display sizes are becoming common. Public kiosks and advertising billboards come in all sizes, too. The scope for expression has broadened considerably.

We're also in the first wave of wearable connected devices. Fitness bands and smart watches have become popular. But that's not all. We're moving into the realm of smart homes,[6] cities,[7] and devices.[8] Health monitors, automobile display panels, entertainment control systems, and virtual and *augmented reality* headsets are finding their places in design, service, repair, gaming, and medical fields. Networked thermostats, smoke/fire/burglar alarms, household appliances, furniture, clothing – even toothbrushes – are on the way, whether we think we need them or not.

> Content is just as much a part of the product as anything else.

Some of these devices have high-resolution screens; others have low-resolution screens that appear large because of their proximity to the eye. Some have no screens of their own and must pair with a device that does. Some don't need a screen at all – they just exist in the realm of interconnected things (more on that in the section titled "Adapting content for the Internet of Things" (p. 72)).

---

[5] eMarketer.com, "2 Billion Consumers Worldwide to Get Smart(phones) by 2016"[32]

[6] Don Clark, "The Race to Build Command Centers for Smart Homes"[21]

[7] Anna Ponting, *High-Tech Urbanism: The Political and Economic Implications of the Smart City*[60]; Cisco Systems, "IoE-Driven Smart City Barcelona Initiative Cuts Water Bills, Boosts Parking Revenues, Creates Jobs & More"[20]; and Dr. Ellie Cosgrave, et al., "Delivering the Smart City"[25]

[8] "10 smart home features buyers actually want"[37]

The number of mobile devices on the market is staggering. In addition to the increasing number of devices in the Apple ecosystem, there are over 18,000 different Android devices on the market right now, and the number is growing.[9] There are commonalities between all of these devices, of course, but even so, there are many differences (screen sizes, screen resolutions, device capabilities, etc.). We can't continue to hand-craft content for each device or even each class of devices. We have to streamline and automate the process.

Each of these devices has its own needs and special requirements. Content created to be viewed on a specific device is doomed to be viewed only on that device. That's no way to create content. It's old fashioned, and it doesn't serve us, our content, or our readers well.

Content is just as much a part of our products as anything else. We build most everything else we sell using automation, why not our content?

If our goal is to future-proof our content by automating its assembly, then we have to start thinking like a manufacturer.[10] We need a manufacturing process with components we assemble. As with manufacturing processes, we will use modular, reusable components to manufacture products. Our content components can be assembled into a wide variety of outputs to meet both our business needs and the needs of our customers. And those small pieces of content, those intelligent content components, are at the heart of intelligent content.

[9] Zach Epstein, "500? 1,000? You'll never guess how many different Android devices are available"[33]

[10] Matt Ball, "Benefits of Modular Construction: It's Like Big Legos"[13]

CHAPTER 9
Building Blocks: The Content Perspective

> Intelligent content is designed to be modular, structured, reusable, format free, and semantically rich and, as a consequence, discoverable, reconfigurable, and adaptable.
>
> —Ann Rockley

Now that we have a definition, we need to understand what makes content intelligent. This chapter shows how the elements of intelligent content can be used with a concrete example, a structured story.

We begin by considering the characteristics of intelligent content that we introduced in Chapter 1:

- **Modular:** Modularity makes it possible to mix-and-match, filter, and assemble content components into any desired configuration.
- **Structured:** Structure enriches content so that computers can automatically process it.
- **Reusable:** Reusability ensures that modular content is consistent and current wherever it appears.
- **Format free:** Format-free content carries no embedded formatting information, enabling structured content to be prepared automatically for any device type or computing platform.
- **Semantically rich:** Metadata supports *findability* as well as the automatic retrieval, assembly, and dynamic delivery of content.

Modular

Modular content is content that is intentionally created as chunks – or components of content – not as documents. Components are stored in a repository – usually a *component content management system* or CCMS – designed to manage the production and assembly of modular content into content products (documents, web pages, etc.). Components have their own lifecycle (owner, version, status, use) and can be tracked individually or as part of a content product.

Before the advent of intelligent content, writers typically created files (documents, PDFs, web pages). Content was locked up inside of documents. The ingredients of each document – things like facts, figures, statistics, images, tables, quotes, product descriptions, value propositions, processes, and procedures – were difficult (if not impossible) to repurpose without manual intervention.

Chunking or modularizing content (intentionally creating reusable content components) makes content available for reuse by both humans and machines. Modular content components can stand alone, be used as building blocks in various content deliverables, and be tracked as they are reused.

Let's look at a story, a common component in news, entertainment, and marketing. A story could consist of several modular elements, for example, a title, a teaser, a pull quote, and both a short version and a long version of the story being told.[1]

Story structure

- `<story>`
  - `<title>`
  - `<teaser>`
  - `<pull_quote>`
  - `<short_version>`
  - `<long_version>`

Here are a few other examples of modular content components:

- Value propositions
- Procedures
- Corporate descriptions
- Product descriptions
- Recipes
- Frequently asked questions (FAQs)

Modular content extends the usefulness and agility of content.

Structured

Structure enriches content so that humans can easily use it and computers can understand and automatically process it. Structure also provides guidance to those who create content.

Structured content is content that follows a specific pattern. It's content that is predictable. Content that enhances the user experience. Content that engenders consumer confidence and satisfaction.[2] It's content that

---

[1] We use angle brackets (< >) to highlight the elements of a story, which we will call *tags*.

[2] Corrina Liao, "Being Predictable: The First Essential of a Customer Centric Business"[50]

can help users with disabilities.[3] It's content that computers can call to duty in multiple contexts.

While content deliverables (website product pages, lists of frequently asked questions, marketing brochures, annual reports, white papers, eBooks, product documentation, and eLearning courses) can – and should – have specific structures, all types of content can benefit from consistent structure.

Continuing with our story example, the structure of a `<story>` comprises semantically rich content components. Semantic content is meaningful content. It provides distinctions in meaning, allowing both humans and machines to understand what the content is about and what it's not about.

Without intelligent content, most content deliverables are prepared with formatting – not semantic meaning – in mind. Content components are authored in word processing tools (like Microsoft Word) or desktop publishing software (like Adobe InDesign) and labeled with stylistic metadata describing the way content will appear.

For example, a tag called `<normal>` might identify a paragraph of text that immediately follows the `<title>` tag and that adopts a set of formatting properties assigned to it. Notice, the `<normal>` tag tells us nothing about the content itself. There is no way to know what the content tagged as `<normal>` is about.

When intelligent content is added to the mix, we tag content components with semantic meaning as our focus. Style and formatting are separate processes that occur after – not during – authoring. We give components distinct semantic content tags. For example, the `<teaser>` tag might refer to a short, introductory summary, designed to arouse interest or curiosity in the topic that follows. Such a tag clearly spells out what content is about.

From the author's point of view, semantic structure tags provide cues and direction. Structured authoring templates reflect the structure of the content type and show authors how to create content based on the structure.

Semantic content tags tell the author what information should be placed in that location, and by extension, what content should not.

---

[3] "Understanding WCAG 2.0: A guide to understanding and implementing Web Content Accessibility Guidelines 2.0" [81]

| Structure turns content into a data source accessible and actionable by both machines and people. | Structure enables authors to focus on what should be their primary job – creating clear, concise, consistent, and relevant content. Structure provides authoring guidance that can be displayed in templates, ~~ensuring veteran and new writers alike create content in the same way~~ – content that complies with |

writing guidelines and that follows an agreed-upon structure.

Structured content enhanced with semantic metadata is easy to find and reuse. Both humans and computers benefit from the addition of unambiguous semantic tags, allowing, for example, content tagged as a `<teaser>` to be automatically located and published to a web service, app, or reused in many different content deliverables.

Structure combined with metadata turns content into a data source that both machines and people can access and process.

Reusable

Content reuse ensures modular content is consistent and current wherever it appears. Reusable content components live in one place but can be referenced (made to appear as if they live) in multiple places.

Reusable content is auditable. We can track it using software designed to manage content components, which means we can find out where, when, and by whom any component has been used.

Reuse goes hand-in-hand with modular content. We can design components to be reuse-friendly, context-independent chunks of content that can be repurposed, as is, in multiple content products.

There are two basic types of content reuse: manual and automated.

Manual content reuse

The most common approach to reusing content is a manual reuse approach known as the copy-and-paste method. It works this way. The author searches for content in a variety of existing documents, locates the content desired, copies it from the source document, and then pastes it into the target document. Seems simple enough.

However, manual reuse is a bad idea; it is labor-intensive, error-prone, and unnecessarily costly. Content reused via the manual copy-and-paste method relies on the memory of human authors – the same folks who can't keep track of their car keys or who regularly misplace their iPhones.

Decades ago, software developers recognized how inefficient and error prone manual reuse can be. They adopted structured programming practices that let them create reusable software modules. More recently, object-oriented programming has taken software reuse even further.[4]

Content that is manually copied from one document and pasted into another is easy to lose track of. What happens if we need to change or update it? Will we be able to find every place where we reused it? Can we be sure we have the latest version of that content everywhere it should appear? What is the risk to the organization if we are unable to locate and update one occurrence?

Manual copy-and-paste reuse opens the door for unnecessary problems with consistency, which in turn creates a host of negative consequences, from regulatory compliance problems to customer confusion. When the source content changes, all the content products in which the content was manually reused are now inaccurate.

Automated content reuse

With automated reuse, we point to (reference) a single instance of the content we wish to reuse. We don't copy and paste it; we *transclude* it.[5]

Transcluded content automatically appears in any document that refers to it, although the transcluded content is not actually part of the document. Because the content is transcluded, changes made to the source content automatically appear wherever it is reused.

In our <story> example, content components could be automatically extracted and reused in a tweet, a Facebook entry, or testimonial.

Content components could also be automatically reused as building blocks in a larger content deliverable or a family of related content products. For example, the <value_proposition> of a new healthcare app could be automatically reused in:

- A product web page
- A printed brochure
- A video script
- An audio clip
- A sales training slide deck

---

[4] "Cut-and-Paste Programming"[11]

[5] Eliot Kimber, "The Language of Content Strategy: Term of the Week – Transclusion"[49]

Automated content reuse is not limited to reusing identical content in multiple deliverables. Content can be designed for filtering based on context, customer data, or other factors. Reusable content prepared this way is particularly powerful for customer-driven dynamic content.[6]

For example, we could create two distinct `<value_proposition>` statements – one appropriate for an audience comprised of prospects and another for an audience made up of existing customers. Depending on the target audience (prospect versus existing customer) the appropriate `<value_proposition>` statement would be automatically reused.

This flexibility is known as *conditional content*. When the content is published for prospective customers, the content for existing customers is filtered out, leaving only content appropriate for prospective customers. This approach can be used for many different purposes. Our creativity is the only limiting factor.

For example, we could easily provide content in multiple languages, filtering out Spanish language versions when providing content to English language prospects.

We could tag small, granular pieces of content as *variables*. A variable can have one value in one situation and another value in another. We could create a variable to represent a `<product_name>`. That variable could be set to automatically change based on the region or country in which the content will be consumed.

We might also include variables for `<unit_of_measure>` (often different from one region of the world to another), `<currency>` (especially useful in sales, marketing, and eCommerce content). The portions of the content that include variables can be reused in multiple deliverables, just like any other reusable content, but only the `<product_name>`, `<unit_of_measure>`, and `<currency>` (variable content) changes based on the region.

Intelligent content ensures there is a single source of truth for all content.

Intelligent content ensures there is a single source of truth for all content. Automated reuse allows us to treat our content like data, which helps us enforce content consistency, ensure content quality, reduce costs, increase relevancy, improve usability, eliminate duplicate content, and optimize content for dynamic delivery.

---

[6] Scott Abel, "What is Dynamic Publishing, Anyway?"[1]

Format free

Format-free structured content carries no embedded formatting information, allowing content to be automatically mapped to the requirements
of a specific device, output channel, or computing platform.

Today, much of our content is stuck in proprietary formats that don't
allow us to quickly and easily publish it to various output channels. Our
content contains information about styles, fonts and colors. It includes
references to pages and page numbers. It often contains layout information that is specific to one particular output.

To respond to the needs of prospects and customers, content must be
freed from the straitjacket of formatting information. Format-free
structured content can help us produce content products in the most
efficient and cost-effective manner possible.

Structured content can be automatically mapped to a particular style of
output (e.g. <story> looks one way on the desktop web and another
way on mobile devices). Structured, format-free content allows us to
re-skin a website, publish to multiple output formats, simultaneously.
All we need is a different style sheet for each output channel.

Format-free structured content can easily be reused across a wide variety
of outputs, without changing the source content.

Semantically rich

What do we mean when we say intelligent content is semantically rich?
We mean that the content stored in the CMS has more depth than the
actual content itself.

The content needs to have extra information associated with it. This
extra information makes our content intelligent. There are two sources
for this extra information; the first is the content structure, which we
discussed earlier, and the other is metadata.

The semantic structure tags in our content act like metadata. In our
<story>, we have tags such as <teaser> and <quote>. The <teaser>
tag is meaningful for both authors and for computers. The computer
treats them as metadata. It can recognize, process, and apply styles for
different channels, all based on the tags in our content.

Metadata is more direct. We apply *labels* (also called attributes) to our
content to provide information about that content. We can label content

components with information such as what product the content is associated with, what language it's in, or what the audience is.

Content components can be labeled in many ways, and we can apply multiple metadata labels to the same component. If we ask the CMS to find all of the elements identified as being in the French <language> where the <country> has been assigned as Canada, we won't get content designed for France or Switzerland even though French is spoken in both of those countries.

Metadata for the <story> could include:

- Product
- Market
- Role
- Region
- Language
- Other

By adding semantic richness to our content (facilitated by both the structure and metadata) we can do all sorts of useful things that we could not do using traditional approaches, such as:

- **Include or exclude content:** We can conditionally include or exclude content components depending on the situation. For example, we might decide to hide the <short_version> of a <story> whenever we display the <long_version>.
- **Extract content:** We could extract the <pull_quote> and put it into a tweet, or we could add it to the <short_version> of the story and post the combination to Facebook.
- **Use specific content:** We could automatically find and use a country-specific logo depending on the assignment of the <country> metadata.
- **Display content in different ways:** We could display content one way on the desktop computer and another way on a smart phone.

A semantically structured story

Figure 9.1 through Figure 9.3 illustrate the building blocks of intelligent content, using the structured <story> we have been discussing.[7]

---

[7] Although the concepts are real, the details of this example (names, situation, etc.) are fictional.

Figure 9.1 – The elements of a semantically structured story as an author would see them

Teaser posted to Twitter   Short version on Facebook

Figure 9.2 – Contents of the `<teaser>` and `<short_version>` tags posted to Twitter and Facebook

Diabetes can be beaten

I put on weight with my second child, but it wasn't too bad; however it just wouldn't come off after my son was born. Even worse I just seemed to keep gaining weight. I was exhausted, irritable, and suffering from anxiety attacks. The doctors said it was probably just a mild case of post-partum blues and not to worry the weight would come off in time. Ya, right!

Well it didn't come off in time, I just kept packing it on and even though I was careful with what I ate it didn't seem to help! My panic attacks got worse, I seemed to be angry all the time and the littlest thing set me off. I was totally depressed. One day I fainted at work. Finally a doctor listened to me, "there was something more wrong with me." After a barrage of tests I was diagnosed with type 2 diabetes.

I have tried to watch my diet, but there never seems to be enough time to make a good meal at night before rushing out the door again with the kids, and by the time evening comes I'm too tired to make lunch for the next day. On the weekend we were at the semifinal soccer game with our daughter. Her team won so she ended up playing two more games. However, I hadn't brought enough food with me, and the food at the concession at the game was abysmal. I got up between games and passed out! Again! One of the other Moms who came to my rescue and with some orange juice to help me get my blood sugars up again started talking about the glycemic index. We talked for hours through the games. I went home and tried it out. It worked, my blood sugars came down, my weight dropped off and I felt so much better. It was surprisingly easy to follow. That was it, the glycemic index was my key to health.

Figure 9.3 – `<long_version>` extracted and published to a website

All of the steps in this example can be performed automatically, as long as the content is structured according to the `<story>` template.

CHAPTER 10
Building Blocks: The Technology Perspective

> Intelligent content is designed to be modular, structured, reusable, format free, and semantically rich and, as a consequence, discoverable, reconfigurable, and adaptable.
>
> —Ann Rockley

Technology (software) plays a big part in the success of every intelligent content project. We need software to help us create, manage, and deliver intelligent content. We need it to help us govern, filter, assemble, and publish our content and to make it accessible anywhere, anytime, on any device.

Let's look at the technology we use to manage and author content from the perspective of the building blocks of intelligent content:

- Modular
- Structured
- Reusable
- Format free
- Semantically rich

Content management

To implement an intelligent content project, we need, at a minimum, appropriate authoring tools and a content management system (CMS).

It's hard enough to keep track of document- or page-based content, and reusing modular content increases the complexity substantially. Managing thousands of content components and orchestrating their creation, management, and delivery requires substantial effort, more effort than we can manage without the assistance of a content management system designed for the task.

To have the best chance for success, our content management system must include at least these capabilities:

- Access control
- Version control
- Workflow support
- Collaborative review

But the capabilities of a standard content management system are not enough. We need much more than a run-of-the-mill CMS to manage intelligent content. We need a component content management system (CCMS) designed to help us manage modular, structured, reusable, format-free, and semantically rich intelligent content.

A CCMS is designed to manage reusable chunks of semantically rich, structured content at the component level, as opposed to the document or file level. A CCMS is required for intelligent content projects.

Our CCMS must provide support for the five characteristics of intelligent content defined in Chapter 1:

Modular, component-based content

Modules are typically referred to as components. Components are chunks (also called elements) of content that vary in size. Some components will be as large as a <topic> (title plus paragraphs, lists, graphics, etc.) while others may be as tiny as a fragment (a paragraph, sentence, phrase, or even one word). We need a component-based tool that allows us to locate, retrieve, tag, and review components whatever their size.

Structured content

Content management systems that store – but do not understand – structured content aren't good enough. Intelligent content requires a CCMS that can recognize the structure of our content and its semantic metadata and then process it using our business rules.

For example, let's say we have created a <story> using a structured content template. A traditional content management system could store the <story> as a file, but it could not determine, for example, which part of the content was the <teaser>. And it could not act upon it (for example, publish it to Twitter or reuse it in another content deliverable). Content stored as a file is a black box – a solid chunk of content that a traditional content management system cannot process intelligently.

To deliver intelligent content, or CCMS must recognize and process structured content.

Reusable content

To make the most of content reuse, we must be able to define the level of granularity – the size of the content components intended for reuse. And our content management system must be able to reuse content at various levels of granularity.

To achieve the productivity and cost savings intelligent content enables, we must be able to easily locate and select the content we need, then reuse it by transclusion in the content product we are creating. Effective

> A CMS must be able to reuse content, regardless of its size.

reuse strategies require a component-based content management system that allows authors to locate content and reference it directly without having to jump through a series of development hoops. Unsophisticated content management systems might require users to determine the unique ID of a piece of content in order to reuse it. Systems designed for intelligent content are designed for productivity and usually provide more elegant support for reuse (e.g., a drag-and-drop interface).[1]

Some CCMSs provide a report that indicates where content has been reused. They also report the percentage of content reuse across a set of content products.

Format-free content

We live in a WYSIWYG (What You See Is What You Get) world. Authoring tools such as Microsoft Word allow authors to format the text so it's visually attractive. But content that is visually attractive for one channel is not necessarily useful for another. Our CMS should allow authors to preview content as it would appear in multiple channels.

Semantically rich content

Most content management systems let authors add metadata to content, but we need to make sure that we can add metadata at any level of content (document, page, topic, fragment, variable). The CMS must recognize and interpret metadata wherever it appears in your content.

For example, let's say we want to publish our <story> but position it differently for two distinct audiences. The <story> would remain the same, but we might want to use a different <quote> in each of the renditions to meet the specific needs of the target audience.

---

[1] Even though a drag-and-drop interface might appear, on the surface, to be the same as the manual cut-and-paste method, behind the scenes, a capable CCMS will automate reuse.

The CMS interprets the component and element-level metadata upon publication. For example, when the `<story>` is published for audience group one, the second `<quote>` is filtered out. When the `<story>` is published for audience group two, the first `<quote>` is filtered out.

Metadata can be used to filter out any content element (images, charts, tables, text, video, etc.).

Authoring

Authors are accustomed to working with word processing tools like Microsoft Word. Word processors allow them to create content rapidly, format it as they see fit, and organize it in an ad hoc manner. Content is created in much the same way using web content authoring tools, with one major difference: Website designers use style sheets to control the look and feel of web pages to ensure consistency of presentation from page to page.

Like web pages, intelligent content separates content from formatting information. But, the authoring tool we require needs to do more than prevent the authors from formatting the content. It must also support the creation of modular, structured, reusable, format-free, and semantically rich content. We need authoring tools that guide authors in the creation of intelligent content. Look-and-feel will be controlled by stylesheets (designed by visual professionals) and applied when the content is published.

Just as we need a different type of content management system, we also need a different type of authoring tool, a structured authoring tool designed specifically to help us easily create structured content.[2]

Modular component-based content

Intelligent content is modular content. Authors need the ability to create components of intelligent content, not documents. However, they also need to see how the components they are creating will fit into the content products being assembled. This means that the structured authoring tool we select must enable authors to both assemble modular content components in a particular order and view those components in context.

---

[2] Rick Yagodich, *Author Experience*[82]

Structured content

Word processing tools give authors a set of style tags (Normal, Heading 1, Heading 2, Heading 3, etc.) to help them format content. But, intelligent content requires us to separate content from formatting information. Instead of style tags, the structured authoring tool we select must allow authors to select and apply structural tags to content.

Structure follows a pattern. Our structured authoring tool should guide the author toward the creation of consistently structured intelligent content that complies with our structural rules.

It should also provide writing cues, such as automatically selecting the next structural tag based on our rules, and allow us to add on-screen authoring instructions. For instance, our structured authoring tool could allow us to provide writing tips and other guidance in-line, ensuring that everyone understands exactly what we mean when we say, "Write a 110-character summary of the story that piques the customer's interest and leaves them wanting to learn more." Authoring guidance helps eliminate guesswork and reliance on memory. And it saves time and ensures that our content is both well structured and well written.

Reusable content

Our structured authoring tool should make it easy for authors to locate and to reuse content. It should do this using functionality, such as a drag-and-drop interface, that authors are already familiar with.

Format-free content

Word processors like Microsoft Word give us a WYSIWYG view of our content. Structured authoring tools can provide a view that resembles WYSIWYG, but is actually an approximation of one potential output. That's because we won't know what the content will look like to the end-user until we publish it. When we're ready to publish, we apply style sheets to get the desired formatting for each channel.

Although the view provided by a structured authoring tool is not an exact representation of the finished content product, it does provide a visual, contextually relevant preview that shows authors how the content is organized and how it will be presented

The structured authoring tool we select should also provide a tags-on view. This functionality lets authors see the structural tags and metadata with the content. For example, with the tags-on view, an author could see that a paragraph of text is tagged as a `<teaser>` and, therefore, understand what type of content to use at that location. When authors unaccustomed to structured content encounter the tag view for the first time, they may feel overwhelmed with detail. But as they become used to creating intelligent content, they adjust to the new ways of working.

Semantically rich content

Metadata can be added to content as it is saved to the CCMS. But, it's better to add metadata to our content as we author it. The structured authoring tool we select must allow authors to add metadata at any level of the content, and it must provide support for tagging conditional and variable text.

We should include metadata labels in our structured authoring templates along with instructions on what information we require in those labels. This will help ensure that authors know what metadata we require, and it will make it easier for authors to add that information as they write.

CHAPTER 11

Case Study: Investment Bank Increases Sales and Reduces Campaign Development Time

A large national bank rolled out a marketing campaign designed to attract prospects to its new investment services offering.

The bank had considerable experience implementing marketing campaigns, but their process was time-consuming, error-prone, and expensive. Three teams created content: a web team, a print team (brochures and flyers), and a customer support team. The web team worked with product development to understand new products and their key positioning points. An external agency developed the print materials, working with the in-house marketing team.

Although the marketing team tried to ensure consistency between web and print content products, it was nearly impossible to detect variations and harmonize the content. That's because web and print content was created by two different teams. These silos prevented the bank from providing a consistent customer experience, leading to customer confusion, complaints, and missed opportunities.

In addition to damaging the customer experience, content silos made it challenging for bank employees to stay on top of changes. For example, customer support staff complained that they learned about new product launches from their customers, not from the bank. When a new product was launched, support would receive calls from customers asking about the new offerings, which support knew little or nothing about.

To compete in a crowded marketplace, the bank needed a better approach. Enter intelligent content.

The bank decided to focus its initial effort on developing a solution designed to attract prospects from their consumer line of business. They targeted 13 different consumer markets and created personas for each group. As a pilot, the bank created intelligent content to target individual investors aged 25 to 34. The persona for these consumers included these characteristics:

- Starting out in life (e.g., new career, marriage, home, family)
- Limited assets to invest (<$30K)
- No retirement financial planning

To promote the importance of investing early, the bank planned to create the following content products for these consumers:

- Direct mail marketing material
- Website (desktop and mobile)
- Other sales and marketing collateral
- Customer support material

Then they created a cross-departmental team to analyze content samples from three previous campaigns to get a sense of the scope of the project. The team identified content products for the campaign, and they worked with support to identify customer needs.

Identifying the necessary content products gave them a goal, but it did not give them the intelligent content strategy they needed to reach that goal. To develop that strategy, they created the following:

- A customer journey map to identify the types of content required at each point in the journey
- Content models to identify common content
- A strategy to automate content reuse
- A taxonomy to support content retrieval
- A process for handing off content to the print team and synchronizing content changes

They developed the campaign as a coordinated whole. The intelligent content strategy ensured that the customer had the right content at the right time and in the content product of their choice. It also ensured that customer support had all the relevant materials in advance of the campaign launch.

The results? The campaign was a tremendous success. Sales increased 25%! Intelligent content enabled the bank to ~~reduce development time by three weeks com~~pared to previous campaigns, pri~~marily through reuse and automated multi-channel delivery~~. Ca~~ll volume was reduced by 10%~~ by providing pin-pointed personalized experiences for customers, and call center support was optimized by ensuring that support staff had customer-facing content well before it was launched for the customer. It didn't take long to convince management that they needed intelligent content for all future marketing campaigns.

CHAPTER 12

Case Study: Medical Device Company Slashes Production Time and Translation Expenses

The diabetes division of a medical device company was struggling with its content on a variety of fronts. The company was a successful producer of blood glucose meters (glucometers) and an insulin pump. They sold different versions of their products for different audiences in different countries around the world. Because the company was global, they had to ensure that any improvements made to their content lifecycle would not cause the company to run afoul of regulatory compliance requirements, which differ from country to country.

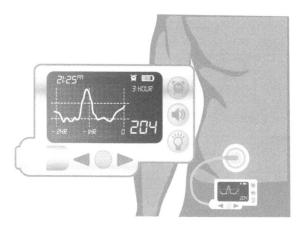

Figure 12.1 – Insulin pump

To meet the diverse needs of these audiences, the company produced versions of their content that varied in language, cultural conventions, and locale details. These factors were often independent. For example, the company produced one version of their content for patients in the United States that used units (weight in milligrams, temperature in degrees Fahrenheit, and 12-hour times) appropriate to that locale, and another version – still in English – that used units (mmol, Celsius, and 24-hour times) appropriate for English-speaking customers who live in countries that don't use the U.S. measurement system.

Similar approaches were taken to address variations in language from locale to locale (e.g., Latin American Spanish versus Castilian Spanish).

The company produced a variety of content products, including product user guides, posters, quick-start cards, instructional materials, and package inserts.

Before intelligent content, they created content using Microsoft Word, then manually copied that content (using the copy-and-paste method) into Adobe InDesign. When they developed a new version of an existing product, they used a PDF of the existing content products to find the differences in content between the existing version of the device and the new version. The authors marked up the existing content with suggested changes, and then someone went into each individual content product and made each change manually.

As a result, the review process was labor-intensive. They held two or three review cycles, and after each review, someone had to edit the content in Adobe InDesign. Then, three separate people read the updated content to make sure that the suggested changes were incorporated and that no other mistakes had been introduced into the content during the process. They had to repeat the process for each language, copying and pasting translated content manually from Word into InDesign.

Product images were also challenging to manage. The company created glucose meter screen images to accompany the text by photographing the actual screens on the device. Each time they needed a screen image, it would have to be photographed. And each photograph needed to be taken multiple times to provide photos for each combination of language and locale. For example, for English, they needed to create photos showing different units of measurement and different time systems (24-hour clock and 12-hour clock).

Beyond the unnecessarily expensive and laborious content maintenance process, the company faced the following additional challenges:

- Regulatory changes required the company to adjust content labels for different locales. For example, content labeled as a <warning> in one jurisdiction was called a <caution> in another, even though the content of the statement remained unchanged.
- They needed to support nine additional languages.
- Timeframes between product launches were becoming shorter.
- They launched a rebranding process estimated to take years and require content changes in thousands of locations.

The process began with a *content analysis* designed to identify:

- The semantic structure of each existing content product
- Opportunities for content reuse
- Content inconsistencies
- Variations in regulations

After the analysis, they developed a content strategy that included the following components:

- Reuse strategy
- Structured content models
- Structured writing guidelines
- Taxonomy
- Workflow

Once they had their content strategy in place, they selected software tools and implemented processes for creating, managing, and reviewing content. Content flowed from the authoring environment into structured templates, which were maintained in a component content management system (CCMS), which became the single source of truth for all content.

They created structured templates that used semantic labels, such as `<caution>` or `<warning>`, rather than stylistic labels, such as `<italic>` or `<bold>`. To accommodate text expansion and contraction, which can occur with translation, they developed language-specific versions of all structured templates.

Adobe InDesign, which had previously been used as both an editing tool and a formatting tool, became a formatting tool only. Authors edited all content in the content management system. They published content through InDesign, but they no longer used it as an editor.

Reuse and automated publishing best practices helped the team reduce its content production time by 30% and the cost of translation by 45%. Reuse and automated publishing also helped eliminate human error.

As an added bonus, the team reduced the implementation time for their rebranding project from 1 year to 6 weeks; an 8-fold improvement. Rather than fighting with the mechanics of every-day tasks, the writers and designers became more productive and more focused on their areas of expertise and the value that they brought to the process. Management was very happy with the results. Today, other product teams are clamoring to adopt intelligent content, too.

CHAPTER 13
Case Study: HMO Increases Revenue and Customer Satisfaction

A large Health Maintenance Organization (HMO) was experiencing problems effectively communicating with and supporting the member organizations that purchased their benefit plans. In the face of increased competition, they knew they had to tackle two critical content challenges.

The first challenge was creating content for two audiences: the Human Resources (HR) team and the employees covered by the benefit plans. The member organizations wanted to integrate the HMO benefit plan content directly into their systems to allow employees to go to one place for all HR information. And they wanted that information to answer as many employee questions as possible, minimizing the need for customer support.

The second challenge was a lack of appropriate content. The HMO had an employer's guide and a benefit plan guide, but these documents were not effective in reducing calls to the customer support hotline. Customer service representatives found themselves creating unique responses to each question and then recreating those same responses when faced with the same question again because they couldn't find the original responses.

Realizing they had both an internal content management issue and an external customer service issue, the HMO decided to analyze their content and content production processes. They assessed the content on their website, in member guides, in *Frequently Asked Questions* (FAQs), and in recent customer email responses. Then, they addressed their content challenges using intelligent content.

First, they analyzed the structure of their FAQs and customer email responses, and then they designed and structured their content so that when they responded to a customer query, they could easily reuse the response in a FAQ on their website. In turn, the FAQs could be reused in customer responses. Having a common structure eliminated the need to rewrite content to address both needs.

Second, they modularized the content locked inside the employer's guide and the benefit plan guide. Employee materials were structured as a subset of the organizational materials so that there was only one place for employees to look for all content related to their benefits. This optimized content creation and simplified content usage.

They tagged each content component with metadata that identified the role, audience, region, and benefit type for that component. They then published content using a dynamic delivery engine that used customer profiles, a customer configuration database, and an organizational database to identify which benefit plans and options matched the member organization and the individual employee of that organization. Figure 13.1 shows the wireframe for the project

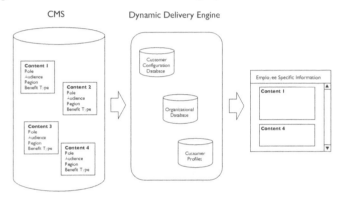

Figure 13.1 – Wireframe for HMO project

By combining organizational and employee data, the HMO could give each employee a personalized content experience, including that employee's specific plan and benefit options.

Once the dynamically configured website was running smoothly, member organizations could provide this content to their employees on their corporate website. A visual *skin* was overlaid on the content based on employee login credentials. This let organizations customize access to benefit and eligibility content for each employee. Figure 13.2 shows sample content displayed using two different skins.

The move to intelligent content resulted in increased productivity and optimized content through content reuse. Customer satisfaction increased through personalized dynamic delivery supported by structured, semantically tagged content. This resulted in fewer customer questions and increased revenue.

Figure 13.2 – Content displayed with two skins

CHAPTER 14
Possibilities

Modular, structured, reusable, format-free, and semantically rich intelligent content increases our capabilities. It empowers us to direct content to work on our behalf and deliver the most value possible. Once we develop intelligent content, we can leverage it in many ways. Let's look at a few of the things that intelligent content makes possible.

Adapting content based on location

Location is an important, but often overlooked, consideration in content improvement projects. Some content is most valuable when it can be tied to a specific place. If we want to provide content that is fine-tuned for a location, we need to know where the device and, presumably, its owner are located. There are a wide variety of technologies to help us leverage location in customer content experiences.

GPS can determine location within 20 feet or so. This is adequate for most purposes, but if we're traveling and using a GPS satellite navigation application with a smartphone, the app will assume we're on the nearest road and display our location accordingly, even if we're actually in a field next to the road.

Often, this is close enough. However, when knowing roughly where our customers are located isn't enough, we need a higher degree of accuracy.

Marketers understand this. Witness the iBeacon,¹ Apple's proprietary hardware that's designed to identify the location of a smartphone within a few inches.² The iBeacon is intended to be used inside malls and stores – places where GPS and cellphone triangulation work poorly, if at all.

This level of location detail can be important if we want to send notifications to prospects and customers based on their exact location. It might be important for us to know that our prospect is browsing in aisle one – the perfume section – and not aisle two, next to the watches.

But it's not only marketing and sales departments who are interested in knowing where customers are when they need content. Anyone whose

---

https://developer.apple.com/ibeacon/

² iBeacon Insider, "What is iBeacon? A Guide to Beacons"[47]

information is location-specific can benefit from providing location-aware content.

Imagine a telecommunications service technician arriving at a cellular transmitter site. She has a laptop, tablet, and mobile phone in addition to her test and troubleshooting gear. As she arrives at the site, she receives a notification that there's a service bulletin that should be applied to a piece of equipment at the site and that a copy of the service bulletin has been automatically pushed to her tablet.

She didn't have to check for the bulletin. When she arrived at the site, the system received her location from her cell phone and triggered a process to determine if there were any updates, fixes, or engineering bulletins relevant to the equipment at that site. The system found a relevant service bulletin, sent her email, and pushed a copy of the service bulletin to her tablet.

Only intelligent content can provide that level of user friendliness.

Adapting content based on user history

When we search for information on the web, advertisements related to our search activity follow us around the web for a while. That's an example of user-based content delivery.

Brands that want to target us can learn a lot about our interests with the help of *cookies* — small text files that websites store in our web browsers to track our digital body language; our movements as we navigate the web. Cookies remember useful things — like login credentials, user preferences, and where we left off on our previous visits. They can also be customized to perform other functions.

Brands use website cookies to make deductions about our interests and intent, and to display content (most commonly, advertisements for products or services) they hope we will be interested in.

While this approach can be irritating to some, most consumers say they find this type of content personalization helpful. In fact, according to a recent study, 71% of American online consumers value content experiences that are based on their web browsing behavior.[3] Connecting insights about prospects and customers with intelligent content allows us to adapt our content to individual prospects and existing customers

---

[3] Listrak, "Survey Reveals 80% of Email Readers Find It Useful When Emails Feature Recommended Products Based on Past Purchases"[51]

alike. Providing personalized content experiences is one of the biggest and most valuable benefits of adopting intelligent content. As data sources become available (and our ability to process and make sense of them improves) the possibilities for personalized intelligent content content delivery will increase.

Adapting content based on user data

Intelligent content makes it possible for us to use information about prospects and customers to help us provide better content to them. One valuable source of information is a user profile.

Profiles can help us determine if a target is a prospective client or an existing customer. Based on that information, we can tailor our content to meet their needs.

We can give prospects content designed to build confidence and trust. The type of content needed during this stage of the customer journey is not the same needed once a prospect becomes a customer, and a new customer will have different needs than a long-term customer. We don't need to provide basic pre-sales information to existing customers. Instead, we can provide content (how-to videos, examples, troubleshooting) that is specific to the product purchased and appropriate for where that customer is at that point in the customer journey.

Intelligent content can allow us to target individuals with links to additional information on new, related, or updated products and services that are tailored to that customer's needs.

Adapting content for multi-channel display

There are two types of device-based content: *responsive* and *adaptive*. They're similar, but not the same.

Responsive design refers to a capability that lets you display content differently depending on the output device. Once a radical concept, responsive design is now the accepted best practice for delivering content on the web. Responsive design is focused on displaying content in the best possible way on any given device (see Figure 14.1).

Figure 14.1 – Responsive design

Responsive design is a subset of *Adaptive design*, which is an approach for enhancing the usability or capability of content on a given device.

Adaptive content adjusts to the needs of the customer, responding not only to the screen size and orientation of the device, but also to the capabilities of the device the customer is using. Adaptive content automatically configures itself to provide content that aligns with device capabilities such as location (GPS), direction (compass), date/time, light sensor, etc.

The possibilities that adaptive content provide us to enhance customer experiences are almost endless. Adaptive content is limited only by our design decisions, the capabilities of the device being used, and the intelligence of our content.

Adapting content for the Internet of Things

The concept of the *Internet of Things* (IoT) has been around for some time, but with today's technology it's finally set to become a reality.

According to Jacob Morgan, writing in Forbes, The Internet of Things "is the concept of connecting any device with an on-and-off switch to the Internet (and/or to each other). This includes everything from cell phones to coffee makers to washing machines to headphones to lamps to wearable devices and almost anything else we can think of."[4]

---

[4] Jacob Morgan, "A Simple Explanation of 'The Internet Of Things.'"[53]

Morgan goes on to say, "The analyst firm Gartner says that by 2020 there will be over 26 billion connected devices…that's a lot of connections (some even estimate this number to be much higher, over 100 billion). The IoT is a giant network of connected 'things' (which also includes people). The relationship will be between people-people, people-things, and things-things."

We are already switching from dumb devices to smart devices or smart things. Smart devices are just like the devices we have now, except they contain sensors and communications equipment that allow them to respond to the environment and communicate over the Internet with each other and with us. They don't have to be close to each other. They don't have to be made by the same manufacturer. All they need is an internet connection, and they can become part of the Internet of Things.

Consumers are aware of some of these smart products. And they are installing everything from small devices, such as the Google Nest thermostat, to complete home automation systems.

Not all smart things are devices consumers interact with directly; many remain hidden and anonymous, doing their business in the background without being noticed.

A familiar example from the last decade is the Tire Pressure Monitoring System (TPMS), which is installed in all new cars sold in the U.S. after September 2007. The system monitors tire pressure and communicates with the driver via a dashboard light or warning sound if the pressure drops to an unsafe level. TPMS systems can also inform the car dealer or manufacturer through a wireless communication system built into the car. Most of the time, such systems remain unnoticed.

However, even systems such as these require some form of documentation, if only for the people who design applications for them, install them, update them, configure them, repair them, or train others to use them. Consumer devices will be noticeable in the more traditional way and will require all sorts of design/installation information, user instructions, and marketing collateral to bring users and devices together.

Unlike traditional, unconnected devices, where printed content accompanies the product or is delivered to a different device in PDF or HTML format, a device attached to the Internet of Things can contain its own content, update that content on the fly, or download content that's specific to the device, its location, or its operation. Handcrafting information for multiple devices is impractical. Intelligent content can help us manage and deliver the right content to each device.

The possibilities are virtually limitless

The possibilities provided by intelligent content are virtually limitless. Every organization that adopts intelligent content does so for one reason: to add capability. They want to do something they couldn't do before. Organizations that have been using intelligent content for several years have found they can leverage their content in ways they never imagined.

Here are a few more capabilities intelligent content makes possible:

- **Adapting content for voice command systems:** Intelligent content makes it possible to provide machine-readable content that can be read aloud by computers. This possibility is attractive to people who need to multi-task (but otherwise have their hands full, like automobile drivers) and to those with visual impairments. As voice-activated interfaces (think Apple's Siri or Amazon's Echo) become commonplace, intelligent content could make it possible for these interfaces to better serve visually-impaired users by encoding additional information for that interface.

- **Adapting content for web services:** Intelligent content can be useful in turning content into a service. What type of service? "A service can be anything and can do anything, as long as the information needed to request it and the work or results that it produces can be effectively described with XML."[5]

- **Enabling automatic publishing:** Intelligent content enables us to schedule publishing tasks to occur automatically. For example, we can instruct our tools to assemble, publish, and deliver content at a specific time and date according to our business rules.

- **Enabling document-to-machine communication:** Intelligent content is both human- and machine-readable. Enabling documents to communicate with machines allows us to ensure that changes in product design or functionality are reflected in up-to-date product content. For example, some smart device manufacturers can integrated updated documentation as soon a design change is finalized.[6]

We can't capture all of the possibilities here, but one thing is certain, once we move to intelligent content, the possibilities are virtually endless.

---

[5] Robert J. Glushko, *Document Engineering*[39]

[6] Alexander Hoffmann, "Smart factories require smart documentation"[45]

CHAPTER 15

Overcoming Objections to Intelligent Content

We get a lot of questions about intelligent content. Of course, sometimes, rather than getting questions, we get "told things" – stories taken out of context or statements repeated by others without factual support. In this chapter we examine and debunk some of the most common objections to intelligent content.

Some of these objections arise from common misunderstandings about factors such as cost (We need how much money?), purpose (Why do we need to change how we work, anyway?), perceived limitations (That's cool, but it will never work for us…), or technology (Why can't we just use the tools we have already?). Other objections are understandable concerns related to change: worries about losing writers, uneasiness about adjusting job descriptions, and so forth.

I'm Marketing, it's just for technical content

I'm in marketing – there's no way this could possibly work for us. This is one of the most common objections and it's fairly easy to dispel.

Marketing content is different from technical or explanatory content in some ways, but at its heart it shares the same need for accuracy, verifiability, and quality. It must be created quickly to meet the needs of the market. It must be interesting, relevant, and engaging. And we must be able to update it rapidly and inexpensively.

Traditionally, marketing content was agile, while technical content was not. Marketing content was highly visual, while technical content was not. Marketing content was engaging and interesting, while technical content was not. Technical content needed sophisticated technology, marketing content did not. See a trend emerging?

In most cases, it is beneficial for technical content to be aligned with marketing content because all content affects the way prospects and existing customers feel about our brand. Therefore, all content is marketing content, regardless of who creates it.

We need intelligent content to unify our content, making it possible to provide a consistent experience across all touch points with our content.

There's no good business reason for creating inconsistent content that damages brand.

In today's global, hyper-connected world, there's no reason to create inconsistent content that damages brand, ruins the customer experience, and wastes finite corporate resources. Marketing must learn to leverage the techniques some forward-thinking technical communication departments have already mastered, techniques that can reduce or eliminate unnecessarily cumbersome, time-consuming, and expensive manual processes; automate content creation, formatting, and publishing tasks; systematically reuse content to meet customer needs; and publish content to multiple channels, simultaneously.

Intelligent content allows us to do all of these things — and everything else we've always done — more efficiently and effectively, affording us the luxury of using the resources saved to innovate.

For instance, intelligent content allows us to create content, and, with the push of a button, republish it in different forms. We can easily re-skin content and know that we're still using the correct/approved content. With intelligent content, we can repurpose marketing content intended for one medium in a totally different medium, depending on the metadata associated with the content and our output requirements. With intelligent content we can reuse, repurpose, and customize our information for different outputs and markets faster and more accurately than ever before.

> Just because content is well-written, displayed in an innovative format, and published in some new and super-cool way, does not make it intelligent content. These things may be attractive, interactive, or amazingly different, but those characteristics don't make content intelligent. Intelligent content relies on repeatable methods, *content standards*, automated processes, and software technology designed to help us create, manage, and deliver relevant, *personalized content* in more efficient and effective ways than traditional publishing approaches allow.

We can't review content in modules; we need content in context

When first encountering the concept of intelligent content, many reviewers, editors, and proofreaders are concerned about the difficulty of properly reviewing content that's broken into reusable components. While they agree that creating modular content for reuse is interesting (and likely advantageous), they argue that reviewing content in sections any smaller than a document is simply impossible.

The actual content review method employed depends on the software tools selected and the implementation details, but in general, during a review cycle, the content under review is displayed in context. Comments made by a reviewer are attached to the content component being reviewed. This same technique is used to provide context to translators.

That said, intelligent content presented for in-context review may not be fully formatted — layout will be minimal. That's not a problem, because we want to focus on improving our content, not the appearance of our content (important though that will be in the final output).

Instead, an approximation of the final content design (images, charts, graphics, text, fonts, colors) will be presented to reviewers during in-context review. For instance, if the text is supposed to be wrapped around an image in the final output, that's unlikely to be visible to the reviewer. For reviewers used to working in desktop publishing environments, not being able to see the final design as they edit and review may introduce some challenges at first, but they usually adjust to this difference as they grow familiar with the approach.

> All content is marketing content, no matter who creates it.

Using visual design as a basis for intelligent content review is a bad practice. It's better to review the content with light styling. That way the content is less likely to be tweaked for a specific appearance by well-intentioned reviewers and more likely to be reusable in multiple contexts.

It's only about reuse

Although intelligent content supports efficient reuse, that's not the only reason to implement the approach. Chapter 4, *The Benefits of Intelligent Content*, discusses other benefits, but even if intelligent content was only about reuse, which it isn't, it would still offer value.

How much content is reusable? We find the average organization that adopts intelligent content enjoys at least 25% content reuse. Depending on the organization and the content, that percentage can be much higher. It can be lower, but it's rarely zero. Managing even small levels of content reuse intelligently is much easier than copy-and-paste.

Content reuse can pay even higher dividends in organizations that translate content into multiple languages. When we reuse content components and their translations, our *return on investment (ROI)* skyrockets. Some organizations report that their biggest savings come from reduced translation costs attributable to content reuse.

It takes too long to implement

It does take extra time to use intelligent content correctly in the early phases, but that's because we have to reengineer our old, outdated processes; adopt new roles, responsibilities, and tools; and learn how to work differently. Moving to intelligent content transforms the way we produce our content, and transformation means big changes involving pushback, uncertainty, fear, rumors, and temporary setbacks the first time through.[1]

The key to success is to correctly identify the scope of the project and clearly understand our objectives. As an intelligent content project rolls out, we will identify new participants and departments who will want to get in on the action. While it's important to encourage widespread participation from all divisions of the organization, we must also avoid expanding project scope. We must address immediate needs first and then, once our systems are up and running, invite other departments to participate.

Take small steps, such as structuring content, first before tackling all the automation, workflow, writing style, and technology changes. Adopting structured, semantically rich content alone will make our content much more effective.

It's too hard to do

Introducing anything new can be a challenge. When creating intelligent content we have to change from a page-based way of thinking about content, to a component-based content paradigm. This is often the biggest challenge, especially for experienced content contributors.

Authors take pride in their work. Traditionally, this has meant that an individual author was responsible for a specific set of deliverables. With intelligent content, authors exchange individual control of deliverables for the flexibility of creating shareable, reusable content products that they develop collaboratively. Rather than being responsible for one content product (or suite of content products) they become responsible for a much broader range of content.

Interestingly, some technical illustrators and graphic artists have adopted component-based content approaches.[2] They've learned to easily create modular components and reuse them where needed.

---

[1] Ron Ashkenas, "We Still Don't Know the Difference Between Change and Transformation"[12]

[2] Matt Sullivan, "Reusable and editable content in Illustrator"[75]

Software developers have been using intelligent content principles, especially component content reuse, since the 1990s.[3] They overcame the "It's too hard to do!" objection by recognizing that the benefits of their approach (they called it object-oriented programming) far outweighed the up-front work required.

It's not about content, we just need new technology

Actually, no. We need some new technology (software) to implement all but the smallest intelligent content project, but that's not our biggest issue. Not by a long shot.

When we move to intelligent content, the biggest challenge isn't software. After all, software doesn't produce intelligent content; we produce it. Software helps us plan, create, manage, and deliver our content, and it helps us do these things efficiently and effectively. Software supports our efforts, but it shouldn't be our focus.

Instead, we must focus on moving to a modular, component-content way of thinking. With intelligent content, we create individual components of content that can be mixed and matched in different ways, for different audiences, which consume content on different output channels. To succeed, we need to collaborate and share information with more people than ever before. And, the way we work (our actual tasks) will change, as will our workflow. We may even need to change the way we define success.

Technology is the easy part. People, and the changes we expect them to make, are often the most difficult obstacles.

> Technology is the easy part; people are the challenge.

Despite the people challenges, moving to intelligent content can be done! The key is to understand what we want to do, when we want to do it, and clearly communicate our goals and expectations to everyone involved in the process, including the naysayers.

Recognizing that this is a cultural change – more than a technological change – and managing expectations is critical to success.

---

[3] Scott Ambler, "A Realistic Look at Object-Oriented Reuse"[8]

It costs too much

There's no question that implementing intelligent content comes with costs. For some organizations it can be cost prohibitive. Software isn't free, and there are associated installation, implementation, and configuration costs. Oh, and there's training. But these costs are common expenses in nearly any transformational project.

Moving to intelligent content is both a cultural and technological transformation. Cultural changes are often harder to make than technological ones, but the cost of technological change can't be dismissed.

The best way to control these costs is to create a well-defined intelligent *content strategy* aimed squarely at helping us accomplish clearly-defined, achievable goals. The best method of keeping costs down is to stick to the project plan. Scope creep increases cost.

Some organizations seem to handle change better when it's introduced in phases. When we break our intelligent content project down into smaller, more manageable chunks, not only is it easier to implement, but cost becomes less of an issue. Expenditures are smaller and the total project budget is spread out over time, making funding such initiatives easier for some, more palatable to others.

Regardless of the approach, it's critical to have a well-researched business case that spells out the potential return on investment from each phase of an intelligent content project. Maintaining momentum is easier when we can prove that the benefits of our efforts far outweigh the costs.

Intelligent content is only for regulated industries

Intelligent content is a particularly good fit for regulated industries. But, intelligent content can provide benefits for nearly every content-heavy organization, regardless of whether it is regulated or not.

When considering a move to intelligent content, organizations in regulated industries are attracted to a variety of benefits, but the primary benefit is improved control over content. Intelligent content is far less likely to be incorrect or outdated when published.

Why? Traditional content production methods rely on outdated content review approaches in an attempt to ensure quality. The traditional approach involves completing a document and then sending it around for review by others. This approach is slow, error-prone, and doesn't align with the agile methodologies many companies are using to drive product development. Quality is often achieved (at least in part) by ensuring that many people get a chance to review the content.

Because we're accustomed to working on a document/page basis, many people feel that the most important review is the final review when the document /page has been completely written and styled. So until they have seen a publication-ready document, they won't sign off on it.

This method was rejected as being too costly and not very effective by the manufacturing sector decades ago. What manufacturers do today is design quality in, and use fewer, but better-targeted quality checks early in the development process. That doesn't mean that reviewers don't look at the final version, they do. However, this final check should require few, if any, changes.

When we adopt intelligent content, we streamline our review process because reviewers can focus on the content without worrying about the fonts, colors, style, and look-and-feel of the final deliverables. This improved focus lowers costs and improves quality.

While regulated industries realize important benefits from intelligent content (quality and content control), all content producing organizations can gain benefit from intelligent content.

We're too small to use intelligent content

This objection has a kernel of truth, but even so, it's not entirely valid.

Not all intelligent content implementations are huge, expensive efforts. We can use the principles of intelligent content – small modular pieces of structured information, early reviews, separating the content from the way it looks – to improve most manual content creation processes.

Many successful projects take place in sizable writing departments in large (often global) companies. These success stories often detail the expansive – and expensive – technology solutions selected by the featured company to make their project a reality. But, intelligent content projects come in all shapes and sizes. Small organizations can also adopt the approach and see sizable benefits.

Guaranteeing success is about choosing the approach, technology, and training that meets the needs of the organization. Not every company that implements intelligent content will require the same plan of attack or the same software tools. There are a variety of tools and technologies, at various price points, that can help us achieve our goals.

Intelligent content can provide even a single writer with benefits worth the effort. We don't need an expensive, multi-seat license to a component content management system to create intelligent content. Some organizations find that small cloud- or server-based systems can empower a small department to create intelligent content. A single writer or small writing team can benefit from being able to easily locate content and know they have the latest version.

The size of the organization is not a determining factor. Don't discount the benefits of intelligent content because of the size of the company.

We're too big to use intelligent content

When we move to intelligent content, we don't have to make all the changes needed at once. In fact, there are many good reasons for adopting a phased approach.

To succeed in a large organization, one of the first steps is to identify influential people in other departments who would benefit from adopting intelligent content. Design an approach that meets their needs. Start small. Identify an individual group to target. Ensure that the type of content they produce can be leveraged by other groups, and make sure the approach works for the initial group before rolling it out to others.

Also, keep in mind that not every group we target will want to join the effort. Some groups won't adopt the new approach, even though it could prove to be useful to them. Other groups might seem like great candidates, but if their current processes are too far away from our reality, including them would be counter-productive. Don't force it!

If there's no business reason to use intelligent content within a particular group, department or organization – don't use it!

Intelligent content requires new technology

This is half true. We can accomplish many of the goals of intelligent content without adopting new technology – at least in the early stages. However, to benefit from all the bells and whistles – automation, sophisticated content reuse, and multi-channel publishing – we need tools to help us create, manage, and deliver intelligent content.

But, there are things we can do to prepare ourselves for the move to intelligent content before we invest money acquiring new technology. The biggest value comes from structuring our content. Analyzing our content and designing a repeatable structure yields more consistent, coherent, streamlined, and effective content.

We don't need special tools to support structure. We can create structured web forms for authoring, or even set up structured content templates in Microsoft Word, before we purchase new technology. As long as authors adhere to the structure of the content and can quickly and easily create content, we can realize significant rewards.

Structured content is not only a best practice, it's required for intelligent content solutions. We need to create, manage, and deliver structured content to realize the full benefits of intelligent content.

I'll lose control/creativity

Control is a myth. On most devices, the reader has ultimate control of fonts, colors, point size, etc. In print, corporate style guides control the look. Intelligent content practices allow us to spend less time with issues, such as look and feel, that we never have had much control over anyway. By spending less time on those issues, we have more time to deal with the aspects of our job where we can be creative. It takes just as much creativity to write structured content as it does to write in stream-of-consciousness mode, and the result will serve the customer better.[4]

---

[4] Rahel Anne Bailie: private communication with Scott Abel

CHAPTER 16
Transitioning to Intelligent Content

In this chapter we provide tips and first steps to help kickstart an intelligent content project.

Let's examine a few recommended first steps. Consider these before attempting to implement intelligent content.

Culture

Adopting intelligent content requires technological change, but these changes are smaller and easier to overcome than cultural changes. As Douglas Adams said in *The Hitchhikers Guide to the Galaxy*[6], "to summarize the summary of the summary, 'people are a problem.'"

The typical response to change is to push back, and if we're trying to change the way we've always done things, we should expect push-back. After all, change can be hard, and it's often uncomfortable.[1] It can even be scary.[2] It breaks our patterns. It erodes our confidence.[3] It makes us feel out of control. But, despite the challenges, change is necessary to make progress.

Human beings are creatures of habit.[4] Even if we realize that the way we work is slow and inefficient, we may not want to change. Even when the work we do is frustrating, we still find ways to rationalize why we should keep working the way we always have. Some behavioral scientists say that we resist change because we are more comfortable with what we know and understand. People who feel this way believe it's better to stick with the devil they know than to make uncomfortable changes.[5]

To succeed, we must educate our stakeholders about the need for intelligent content. And to explain the benefits, we have to first understand the pain. The desire for change is more-often-than-not dependent on pain. According to Pip Coburn, "Users will change their habits when

---

[1] Rosabeth Moss Kanter, "Ten Reasons People Resist Change"[48]

[2] Dino Signore, "Fear Factor: Change Can Be Scary (Leaders Take Note)"[73]

[3] Julia Rains, "Five Reasons People Resist Change"[64]

[4] Grace Boyle, "The Inconvenience of Change: We Are Creatures of Habit"[17]

[5] Joyce E. A. Russell, "How to create change in the workplace"[70]

the pain of their current situation is greater than their perceived pain of adopting a possible solution.[6]

The best way to increase the probability of success is to focus on what executive coach and business strategy consultant Mario Raia refers to as the four Cs:[7]

- **Clarity:** We have a strategy, goals, and a plan. And we have a process to help us achieve our goals.
- **Confidence:** We trust our strategy, plan, process, and people.
- **Competency:** We have the expertise to execute our plan.
- **Collection of past experiences:** We have assessed past experiences, looking for any that might lead us to believe we won't be successful. If so, we have addressed them.

Practical advice: Find out what's causing the team pain today. Make sure the proposed changes will alleviate as much pain as possible. Educate everyone. Evangelize often. Help others see the potential benefits. And, always be honest and forthright about the need for change and its impact on the organization.

Take advantage of existing processes and procedures

Take advantage of existing processes, standard operating procedures (SOPs), and methods of work. SOPs and existing business processes determine what happens when, where, under what circumstance, and by whom. Examine existing SOPs and extract the salient points. If official SOPs don't exist, find out how things work by examining formal and informal processes. Look for things that we must do (for regulatory or valid business reasons) and get rid of those things that aren't essential.

Ensure our new way of working supports the things we need to do, and enables us to eliminate unnecessary processes, halt production of un-needed deliverables, and reduce unreasonable delays.

Practical advice: Build on existing processes, modify these processes to reflect the new way of working. This will make it easier for everyone to transition.

---

[6] Pip Coburn, *The Change Function*[24]

[7] Mario Raia, "Do People Really Resist Change?"[63]

Look for change champions

Change champions help their organizations lead transformation. They must see the vision, understand the goal, and advocate for change. Transformative changes are often dramatic and profound innovations that take an organization in a new business direction, a direction that often bears little or no resemblance to the past way of working.

The first and most obvious change champions are leaders who are visible, strong, and active members of our organization. Champions lend support, provide guidance, and communicate the importance of the change to others. They are often called upon to evangelize the strategy, publicize milestones and achievements, and unify lower level and department management. Champions are especially useful in helping leaders whose departments are interdependent understand that although the changes may be uncomfortable, they are necessary for the organization to achieve its broader goals.

> Transformative changes take an organization in a new direction, one that often bears little resemblance to the past.

To select a champion, look for someone whose organization would benefit from faster delivery of more accurate content. Make sure the potential champion is influential, willing to commit, and high enough on the corporate ladder for their support to carry weight.

If we encounter difficulties recruiting a particularly influential champion, we can try talking to someone who works for our candidate. Explain the benefits of intelligent content and why it would matter to the champion being targeted. Then work together to develop an approach that will appeal to the target champion.

Practical advice: Find out who will benefit from faster delivery of more accurate content. Approach them. Make sure they are influential, willing to commit, and high enough on the corporate ladder (the higher, the better) for their support to matter to others.

Ask the right questions

Implementing an intelligent content strategy and realizing the benefits does not happen overnight. The importance of planning transformative projects ahead of time can't be overstated.

Implementing intelligent content is significant and consequential. There are moving parts, dependencies, people, culture, language, and technology involved. While it would be nice to put everything on hold while we implement, intelligent content projects often must be implemented in parallel with other projects. To transform our organization, we have to manage our current workload, while designing a new-and-improved process for the future.

To determine what needs to change, it helps if we first examine how we work today. The first step is to ask questions, a lot of them.

How do we create content? Who creates it? Who helps? Why do they create it? For whom? Who is collaborating? On what? Who is sharing content? Who could – or should – be sharing content, but isn't? How can we get them involved? Who is in charge of that department? Are we required to produce content for regulatory reasons? Are we required to track metrics, provide an audit trail, or prove we follow our own policies and procedures?

What type of information are we creating? In what languages? In which formats? For what devices? Do we create interactive content? Audio? Video? Multimedia? Do we use any content standards, and if so, are those standards shared across the organization? Does everyone follow the rules? What happens if they don't?

Analysis is time well spent. Without it, our chances of success are greatly diminished.

The analysis phase of an intelligent content project is where we start to see the complexity, understand the dependencies, and get a good idea of where the pain points are. A proper analysis will help us reimagine our processes in the future. Understanding what we do today – and how we do it – will help us uncover the hidden productivity-draining tasks that should be streamlined, automated, or eliminated. Analysis is time well-spent. Without it, our chances of success are greatly diminished.

Practical advice: Talk to everyone involved in content development. Ask them what works and what doesn't. Identify the pain points. Assure everyone that it is important to identify problems so that they can be reduced or eliminated.

Promote possibilities, but don't over promise

Adopting intelligent content is a cultural change. It relies on people, processes, and the power of technology to deliver maximum value. Like any technological project, it's best implemented in a phased manner.

To ensure success, start by identifying short-term goals and work toward achieving them. Resist adding-in more features until after the initial roll-out. Make sure team members understand the importance of getting the basic mechanics working first. Even if a request is simple to fulfill, it can derail the project. Stick to the plan. Nice-to-have is not a necessity. Projects that are controlled and follow a predetermined strategy and plan of attack are far more likely to succeed than projects that get side-tracked by requests for "just one more little feature."

That said, don't discourage team members from suggesting new features and capabilities. Encourage them, but within the confines of existing priorities and the project plan. Don't promise people anything that can't be delivered within a reasonable timeframe.

> Projects that follow a predetermined strategy are more likely to succeed.

Practical advice: Educate everyone to the possibilities, but support them with a business case that demonstrates return on investment. Be conservative. It's better to under-promise and over-deliver.

Select the right first project

Selecting the right first project to begin an intelligent content adventure is extremely important. Picking the wrong project can lead to failure. Don't pick a mission-critical project with a very short deadline; developing an effective intelligent content strategy takes time to do properly. Mistakes will be made (that's guaranteed) and we need time to learn from them. The pressure to perform too quickly may also sabotage the development team's desire to do it right.

To have the best chance for success, pick a project that is certain to show return on investment. The best candidates are projects involving content that already exists, but will require a major revision to meet current needs. The changes required to adopt an intelligent content strategy will be less taxing if the content being structured needs to be updated anyway. And legacy content gives content analysts and information architects real content work with from the beginning.

Practical advice: Start with a project that is not mission critical, but which is large enough to test the design and vision. Avoid projects with significant amounts of new content; stick with projects that mostly have legacy content.

Think big, act small

Thinking big means considering the larger needs of the organization so the solution will meet future needs. Acting small means starting with one area, or one project, and then using the smaller project success to fuel future efforts and to gain experience. Without the knowledge gained from the smaller initiative, we might implement a solution that is too narrow, a mistake that can prove costly later.

Practical advice: Start with a small, manageable project, but talk to anyone who might benefit from intelligent content. That will help ensure that when the time comes to take on a larger project, there will be fewer surprises, and the scope will be better understood. Be agile. Iterate to grow. Don't try to tackle too much with the first project.

Plan ahead – and, plan for changes in our plan

Winston Churchill was reputed to have said, "planning is invaluable, but plans are useless." What he meant was that examining facts, understanding the situation, and evaluating the possibilities are the keys to preparation. However, schedules slip, people leave, new products are created or are moved up in the release schedule. Companies are bought or sold, staff is cut, and new team members are hired. Target markets shift. Nothing is set in stone.

As Louis Pasteur said, "chance favors the prepared mind."[8] Proper early planning can help us manage changes, even unlikely ones.

Practical advice: Think through possible problems. Identify ways to solve them. Enlist the help of the project planning team early in the process. Their experience will prove invaluable.

Communication is key

As we note throughout this book, moving to intelligent content is a significant change that we must discuss and explain in detail. We can't just unveil it at the last minute.

It should go without saying that the project team needs to be in the loop – they *are* the loop, after all. But they're not the only people we need to

---

[8] https://en.wikiquote.org/wiki/Louis_Pasteur

communicate with. We need to keep other interested parties informed. Communication is the key success.

Who do we need to communicate with? It depends on our organization, but typically we need to be talking with anyone who has expressed an interest in improving content quality, accuracy, usability, consistency, or timeliness. These people might not be directly related to our project, but keeping them informed is a great way to build interest in the project.

Create a communication plan designed to get everyone on the same page. Communicate the vision, milestones, expectations, successes, setbacks, and lessons learned regularly. Engage a team member to act as communication manager for the project.

Practical advice: Communicate frequently. Communicate reasons for change, adjustments to the plan, and project updates. Communicate successes and setbacks. Never hide problems. Be open and honest, but have a plan of action. Get change management personnel involved early.

CHAPTER 17
Getting Started with Intelligent Content

Intelligent content is designed to be modular, structured, reusable, format free, and semantically rich and, as a consequence, discoverable, reconfigurable, and adaptable.

Begin by establishing a team (interdepartmental/interdisciplinary) of eager and curious people to lead the initiative. Use this checklist to assist in the development of an intelligent content strategy.

1. Analyze both customer and organization needs. Determine whether intelligent content can help meet those needs.
2. Analyze the content lifecycle, what's working and what's not working. Identify pain points. Determine whether intelligent content can help eliminate the problems.
3. Conduct a content audit to determine how content is used today and how it could be reused in the future.
4. Identify intelligent content capabilities that would improve customer experience and positively affect the bottom line.
5. Develop a vision based on the capabilities intelligent content offers.
6. Determine the return on investment possible from adopting intelligent content.
7. Develop a strategy that includes the following steps:
   - Plan how to modularize content.
   - Develop semantically structured content models.
   - Develop a reuse strategy, identifying what content should be reused, how it will be reused, and how it will be controlled.
   - Identify target content channels. Develop stylesheets appropriate for each channel.
   - Develop semantically rich metadata.
8. Select technology (new or upgraded) to support the project.
9. Develop content best practices and training materials.
10. Develop a change management plan to ensure everyone embraces the vision and understands the new concepts and processes.

Think agile. Iterative steps are the key to success.

References

Cited references

[1] Abel, Scott. "What is Dynamic Publishing, Anyway?" The Dynamic Publisher, 2012. http://bit.ly/1EFYsNL.

[2] Abel, Scott. "Content Marketing Institute Acquires Intelligent Content Conference (ICC)." http://bit.ly/1DVRg5o.

[3] Abel, Scott. "Lip Service is No Longer Enough: Why You Need a Unified Customer Experience Strategy." http://bit.ly/1JbGeZN.

[4] Abel, Scott, and Rahel Anne Bailie, editors. *The Language of Content Strategy*. XML Press, 2014.

[5] Acquity Group. "2014 State of B2B Procurement Study: Uncovering the Shifting Landscape in B2B Commerce." http://bit.ly/1KqxyeQ.

[6] Adams, Douglas. *The Hitchhiker's Guide to the Galaxy*. Pan Books. 1979.

[7] Adobe. "The Personalization Payoff: The ROI of Getting Personal." http://adobe.ly/1Pu9sEd.

[8] "A Realistic Look at Object-Oriented Reuse." Dr. Dobbs, January 1, 1998. http://ubm.io/1huzH2v.

[9] Andrews, Michael. "Should a content strategist learn to code?." Content Strategy Forum, 25 June 2015. http://bit.ly/1DTcpNd.

[10] Anonymous. "L10N Reality Check: Industry Insider Shines Light on the Dirty Little Secrets of the Translation and Localization Industry That You Won't Learn at a Webinar." http://bit.ly/1DVRSbl.

[11] Antipatterns. "Cut-and-Paste Programming." SourceMaking. http://bit.ly/1PoR3rX.

[12] Ashkenas, Ron. "We Still Don't Know the Difference Between Change and Transformation." Harvard Business Review, January 15, 2015. http://bit.ly/1HYZ559.

[13] Ball, Matt. "Benefits of Modular Construction: It's Like Big Legos." lineshapespace.com, 2014. http://autode.sk/1flr6gt.

[14] Beaujon, Andrew. "AP will use robots to write some business stories." http://bit.ly/1HLSdIc.

[15] BizShifts. "Knowledge Workers are the Drivers of Economic Growth: They Require a Different Management Process, and Organizational Structure." BizShifts-Trends, October 2011. http://bit.ly/1hH1OLu.

[16] Bonawandt, Christian. "Your Secret Weapon to Influencing Decision Makers throughout the Buying Process." ThomasNet. http://bit.ly/1gOTM2z.

[17] Boyle, Grace. "The Inconvenience of Change: We Are Creatures of Habit." Life Without Pants, 2009. http://bit.ly/1JlYGdX.

[18] Castellano, William G. "Welcome to the New Normal." Financial Times Press, September 2013. Chapter from *Practices for Engaging the 21st Century Workforce: Challenges of Talent Management in a Changing Workplace.* http://bit.ly/1NzXnfC.

[19] CEB. "Sell How Your Customers Want to Buy." http://bit.ly/1gOTXL3

[20] Cisco Systems, Inc. "IoE-Driven Smart City Barcelona Initiative Cuts Water Bills, Boosts Parking Revenues, Creates Jobs & More." http://bit.ly/1NDkupz.

[21] Clark, Don. *The Race to Build Command Centers for Smart Homes.* Wall Street Journal, January 4, 2015. http://on.wsj.com/1UR9clV.

[22] CMO by Adobe. "Retailers Seek Innovation In Personalization." http://cmo.cm/1IVm0SM.

[23] Content Marketing Institute. "What is Content Marketing?" http://bit.ly/1WxlQIg.

[24] Coburn, Pip. *The Change Function: Why some technologies take off and others crash and burn.* Portfolio, 2006.

[25] Cosgrave, Ellie, Léan Doody, and Nicola Walt. "Delivering the Smart City: Governing Cities in the Digital Age." University College London, 2014. http://bit.ly/1hmb2wW.

[26] Disley, Jan. "Exclusive: Poo Listed on Ham Ingredients." Mirror Online. 2006. http://bit.ly/1TJLDZN.

[27] Dobbs, Richard, et al. "The World at Work: Jobs, pay, and skills for 3.5 billion people." McKinsey & Company Insights & Publications, June 2012. http://bit.ly/1HQC44k.

[28] Drucker, Peter F. "Knowledge-Worker Productivity: The Biggest Challenge." California Management Review, 1999. http://bit.ly/1MsVfHT.

[29] Drucker, Peter F. *Management Challenges for the 21st Century.* HarperBusiness. 2001.

[30] Dupre, Elyse. "80 Percent of Americans Enjoy Purchase-Based Recommendations in Email." Direct Marketing News, 2015. http://bit.ly/1K129Uj.

[31] Eckerle, Courtney. "Offer Relevance: How Edmunds.com achieved an 18% increase in price quote requests through personalized targeted marketing." Marketing Sherpa, 2012. http://bit.ly/1Puaa4m.

[32] eMarketer.com. "2 Billion Consumers Worldwide to Get Smart(phones) by 2016." http://bit.ly/1vVbVjR.

[33] Epstein, Zach. "500? 1,000? You'll never guess how many different Android devices are available." BGR, 2015. http://bit.ly/1flqaZo.

[34] Feldman, Susan, and Chris Sherman. "The High Cost of Not Finding Information." An IDC White Paper, 2007. http://bit.ly/1DYQDYu

[35] Gartner Group. "Gartner Says Less than 10 Percent of Enterprises Have a True Information Strategy." 2013. http://bit.ly/1TL4Mj9.

[36] Gleanster Research. "The $958M Marketing Problem: Quantifying the cost of inefficiency in your content production." http://bit.ly/1LgndHV.

[37] Glink, Ilyce. "10 smart home features buyers actually want." CBS MoneyWatch, April 11, 2015. http://cbsn.ws/1J13vwb.

[38] Glueck, Jeffrey J., et al. "The Service Revolution: Manufacturing's Missing Crown Jewel." Deloitte Review, 2007.

[39] Glushko, Robert J., and Tim McGrath. Document Engineering: Analyzing and Designing Documents for Business Informatics and Web Services. The MIT Press, 2008.

[40] Glushko, Robert J.. "Substituting Information for Interaction: A Framework for Personalization in Service Encounters and Service Systems." Journal of Service Research. UC Berkeley School of Information, October 31, 2012. http://bit.ly/1U00383.

[41] Glushko, Robert J. The Discipline of Organizing. The MIT Press, 2013.

[42] Gschwandtner, Gerhard. "4 Leadership Trends in B2B Sales & Marketing." Selling Power. http://bit.ly/Z08RyM

[43] Freeman, Karen, Patrick Spenner, and Anna Bird. "Three Myths about What Customers Want." http://bit.ly/1MwqTpg.

[44] Hershey, Michelle Blondin. "Hey, Sales & Marketing…You're not Meeting Prospects' #1 and #2 Needs!" http://bit.ly/1WxoX38.

[45] Hoffmann, Alexander. "Smart factories require smart documentation" tcworld, 2015. http://bit.ly/1JbTPQN.

[46] Hussain, Anum. "Personalized Calls-to-Action Convert 42% Better." Hub Spot, 2013. http://bit.ly/1hH2K2o.

[47] iBeacon Insider. "What is iBeacon? A Guide to Beacons." http://bit.ly/1hP9WJS.

[48] Kanter, Rosabeth Moss. "Ten Reasons People Resist Change." Harvard Business Review, September 25, 2012. http://bit.ly/1E95rEd.

[49] Kimber, Eliot. "Term of the Week – Transclusion." Chapter from *The Language of Content Strategy*. XML Press, 2014. http://bit.ly/1gZhwRy.

[50] Liao, Corrina. "Being Predictable: The First Essential of a Customer Centric Business." uxmag.com, 2011. http://bit.ly/1Jdsi1v.

[51] Listrak. "Survey Reveals 80% of Email Readers Find It Useful When Emails Feature Recommended Products Based on Past Purchases." Listrak.com, 2014. http://bit.ly/1JlKdP8.

[52] Michiels, Ian. "Measuring Inefficiency in Your Content Marketing Production Processes." Customer Think, 2015. http://bit.ly/1LewLjR

[53] Morgan, Jacob. "A Simple Explanation of 'The Internet Of Things.'" Forbes, 2014. http://onforb.es/1PCLWFf.

[54] MyBuys. "MyBuys / etailing group Consumer Survey Reveals Customer-Centric Marketing Drives Buyer Readiness and Purchases." 2013. http://bit.ly/1Mwr6c4

[55] New York Times. "The New York Times Innovation Report." 2014. http://bit.ly/1hH30hO

[56] New York Times. "Notable Deaths 2014." 2014. http://bit.ly/1NzY8oX

[57] Nielsen, Jakob. "Progressive Disclosure." Nielsen Norman Group http://bit.ly/1WxyEhZ.

[58] Online Marketing Muscle. "Are You Guilty of Using a 'Spray & Pray Marketing' Approach to Attract Your Target Market?" http://bit.ly/1UIDo2h.

[59] Platt, David S. *Why Software Sucks…and What You Can Do About It*. Addison-Wesley Professional, 2006. http://www.whysoftwaresucks.com.

[60] Ponting, Anna. *High-Tech Urbanism: The Political and Economic Implications of the Smart City. Honors Thesis Program on Urban Studies,* Stanford University, May 13, 2013. http://stanford.io/1URbYri.

[61] Pulizzi, Joe. *Epic Content Marketing: How to Tell a Different Story, Break through the Clutter, and Win More Customers by Marketing*. McGraw-Hill Education, 2013.

[62] Purplefusion. "Remembering a classic: The Wax Machine."
http://bit.ly/1EyhF3U.

[63] Raia, Mario. "Do People Really Resist Change?" LinkedIn, 2014.
http://bit.ly/1WIxqjZ.

[64] Rains, Julia. "Five Reasons People Resist Change." American Express,
December 29, 2011. http://amex.co/1MBKItQ.

[65] Rockley, Ann. "The Impact of Single Sourcing and Technology." *Technical Communication*, May, 2001. Volume 53, Number 4, Pages 189–193.

[66] Rockley, Ann. "Best Practices: Creating a Winning ROI." *The Rockley Report*,
June, 2005. Volume 2, Number 2. http://bit.ly/1Jce0OJ

[67] Rockley, Ann. "What is Intelligent Content?" Relevance. 2008.
http://bit.ly/1NhwRuk.

[68] Rockley, Ann and Charles Cooper. *Managing Enterprise Content: A Unified Content Strategy.* 2nd ed. New Riders Press, 2012.

[69] Rugh, John. "Earn a Customer for Life with Post-Sale Content Marketing."
Relevance, 2014. http://bit.ly/1hgFEjr.

[70] Russell, Joyce E. A. "How to create change in the workplace." Washington
Post, December 1, 2013. http://wapo.st/1E7So5M.

[71] Schiff, Allison. "Direct Mail Response Rates Beat Digital." Direct Marketing
News, June 2012. http://bit.ly/1NcrT1O.

[72] O'Keefe, Sarah. "Calculating the ROI of DITA." 2011.
http://bit.ly/1TKXmqW

[73] Signore, Dino. "Fear Factor: Change Can Be Scary (Leaders Take Note)"
Inc Magazine, January 20, 2014. http://bit.ly/1K9QdQb.

[74] Solis, Brian. "A Critical Path for Customer Relevance, Part 1."
http://bit.ly/1UPkLK8.

[75] Sullivan, Matt. "Reusable and editable content in Illustrator" SlideShare,
July 8, 2012. http://bit.ly/1gZHYdJ.

[76] Swisher, Val. "Intelligent Content Meets Translation." 2015.
http://bit.ly/1TKXpTC

[77] Swope, Amber. "Calculating the Financial Impact of DITA for Translation."
Writing Assistance, Inc. http://bit.ly/1IVqSqW.

[78] Taylor, Glenn. "B2B Content Preferences Survey: Buyers Want Short,
Visual, Mobile-Optimized Content ." DemandGen Report, 2014.
http://bit.ly/1fiNOFU.

[79] Veracode. "Companies Worldwide Are Adopting Agile Development Techniques." 2015. http://vera.cd/1WxnEkK

[80] VersionOne. "8th Annual State of Agile Survey." 2013. http://bit.ly/1Lex2mQ

[81] W3C. "Understanding WCAG 2.0: A guide to understanding and implementing Web Content Accessibility Guidelines 2.0." W3C, 2015. http://bit.ly/1gZg4OU.

[82] Yagodich, Rick. *Author Experience: Bridging the gap between people and technology in content management.* XML Press, 2014.

Recommended Resources

Change Management

Duck, Jeanie Daniel. *The Change Monster.* New York: Crown Business, 2002.

Mulholland, Andy, Chris S. Thomas, Paul Kurchina with Dan Woods. *Mashup Corporations: The End of Business as Usual — A Chronicle of Service-Oriented Transformation.* Evolved Media Network, 2006.

Lencioni, Patrick. *Silos, Politics and Turf Wars: A Leadership Fable about Destroying the Barriers that Turn Colleagues into Competitors.* Jossey-Bass, 2006.

Harvard Business Review. *HBR's 10 Must Reads on Change.* Boston: Harvard Business Review Press, 2011.

Gardener, Howard. *Changing Minds: The Art and Science of Changing Our Own and Other People's Minds.* Harvard Business School Press, 2006.

Heath, Chip, and Dan Heath. *Switch: How to Change Things When Change Is Hard.* New York: Crown Business, 2010.

Kawasaki, Guy. *Enchantment: The Art of Changing Hearts, Minds, and Actions.* Portfolio-Penguin, 2011.

Duhigg, Charles. *The Power of Habit: Why We Do What We Do in Life and Business.* Random House, 2012.

Content Management

Boiko, Bob. *Content Management Bible.* New York: Hungry Minds, 2004.

Content Marketing

Pulizzi, Joe. *Epic Content Marketing: How to Tell a Different Story, Break through the Clutter, and Win More Customers by Marketing.* McGraw-Hill Education, 2013.

Michelson, James D. *Cross-Media Marketing 101: The Concise Guide to Surviving in the C-Suite.* Schooner Press, 2011.

Content Strategy

Abel, Scott and Rahel Anne Bailie, editors. *The Language of Content Strategy.* XML Press, 2014.

Halvorson, Kristina and Melissa Rach. *Content Strategy for the Web.* 2nd ed. New Riders, 2012.

Rockley, Ann, and Charles Cooper. *Managing Enterprise Content: A Unified Content Strategy.* 2nd ed. New Riders Press, 2012.

Land, Paula Ladenburg. *Content Audits and Inventories: A Handbook.* XML Press, 2014.

Kissane, Erin. *The Elements of Content Strategy.* A Book Apart, 2011.

Nichols, Kevin P. *Enterprise Content Strategy: A Project Guide.* XML Press, 2015.

O'Keefe, Sarah S., and Alan S. Pringle. *Content Strategy 101: Transform Technical Content into a Business Asset.* Scriptorium Publishing, 2012.

Whitehead, Jo. *What You Need to Know About Strategy.* Capstone Publishing, 2011.

Leibtag, Ahava. *The Digital Crown: Winning at Content on the Web.* Morgan Kaufmann, 2014.

Mckeown, Max. "The Strategy Book." Pearson Education, 2012.

Customer Experience

Bliss, Jeanne. "Recorded Webinar: How To Build Your Customer-Driven Growth Engine." http://bit.ly/1DZrE7D

Brown, Dan M. *Communicating Design: Developing Web Site Documentation for Design and Planning.* 2nd ed. New Riders, 2011.

Kawasaki, Guy. *How to Drive Your Competition Crazy: Creating Disruption for Fun and Profit.* Hyperion, 1995.

Cooper, Alan. *The Inmates are Running the Asylum: Why High-Tech Products Drive Us Crazy and How to Restore the Sanity.* Macmillan Computer Publishing, 1999.

Rose, Robert, and Carla Johnson. *Experiences: The 7th Era of Marketing.* Content Marketing Institute, 2015.

Bliss, Jeanne. *Chief Customer Officer 2.0: How To Build You Customer-Driven Growth Engine.* 2015.

Marcotte, Ethan. *Responsive Web Design.* A Book Apart, 2011.

Mulder, Steve, and Ziv Yaar. *The User Is Always Right: A Practical Guide to Creating and Using Personas for the Web.* New Riders, 2006.

Dynamic Content

Hackos, JoAnn T. *Content Management for Dynamic Web Delivery.* Wiley Computer Publishing, 2002.

Global Content

Swisher, Val. *Global Content Strategy: A Primer.* XML Press, 2014.

DePalma, Donald A. *Business Without Borders: A Strategic Guide to Global Marketing.* Global Vista Press, 2002.

Governance

Welchman, Lisa. *Managing Chaos: Digital Governance by Design.* Rosenfeld, 2015.

Information Development

Hackos, JoAnn T. *Information Development: Managing Your Documentation Projects, Portfolio, and People.* Wiley Computer Publishing, 2007.

McGuire, Hugh, and Brian O'Leary. *Book: A Futurist's Manifesto: A Collection of Essays from the Bleeding Edge of Publishing.* O'Reilly Media, 2012.

Hackos, JoAnn T., and Janice C. Reddish. *User and Task Analysis for Interface Design.* John Wiley & Sons, 1998.

Intelligent Content

Content Marketing Institute. "Intelligent Content Article Archive," 2014–2015. A compilation of articles about intelligent content. http://contentmarketinginstitute.com/intelligent-content/blog/.

Rockley, Ann. "What is Intelligent Content?" Relevance. 2008. http://bit.ly/1NhwRuk.

Rockley, Ann, and Gollner, Joe. "An Intelligent Content Strategy for the Enterprise." *ASIS&T Bulletin.* Dec 2010/Jan 2011. http://bit.ly/1HU9XkJ.

Gollner, Joe. "The Emergence of Intelligent Content." The Content Philosopher, 2010. http://www.gollner.ca/2010/01/intelligent-content.html.

Gollner, Joe. "The Challenge of Managing Intelligent Content." The Content Philosopher, 2010. http://www.gollner.ca/2010/01/managing-intelligent-content.html.

Gollner, Joe. "Defining Intelligent Content." The Content Philosopher, 2015. http://www.gollner.ca/2015/03/defining-intelligent-content.html.

Internet of Things

Kellmereit, Daniel, and Daniel Obodovski. *The Silent Intelligence: The Internet of Things.* DnD Ventures, 2015.

Markup Languages

Rockley, Ann, Charles Cooper, and Steve Manning. *DITA 101: Fundamentals of DITA for Authors and Managers.* Rockley Press, 2009.

Goldfarb, Charles F., and Paul Prescod. *The XML Handbook.* 3rd ed. Prentice Hall, Inc, 2001.

Maler, Eve, and Jeanne El Andaloussi. *Developing SGML DTDs: From Text to Model to Markup.* Prentice Hall, Inc, 1996.

Dick, Kevin. *XML: A Manager's Guide.* Addison-Wesley, 2000.

Brown, Peter. *Information Architecture with XML: A Management Strategy.* John Wiley & Sons, 2003.

Linton, Jennifer, and Kylene Brusk. *Introduction to DITA: A User Guide to the Darwin Information Typing Architecture.* Comtech Services, 2006.

Kimber, Eliot. *DITA for Practitioners: Volume One (Architecture and Technology).* XML Press, 2012.

Walsh, Norman. *DocBook 5: The Definitive Guide.* O'Reilly Media, 2010.

Meaningful Metrics

Lewis, Mark. *DITA Metrics 101: The Business Case for XML and Intelligent Content.* Rockley Publishing, 2012. https://www.ditametrics101.com

Lewis, Mark. "Recorded Webinar: The ROI of Intelligent Content." https://www.brighttalk.com/webcast/9273/135273

Metadata

Mathewson, James, Frank Donatone, and Cynthia Fishel. *Audience, Relevance, and Search: Targeting Web Audiences with Relevant Content.* IBM Press, 2010.

Glushko, Robert J. *The Discipline of Organizing.* The MIT Press, 2013.

Organizing Information

Glushko, Robert J., and Tim McGrath. *Document Engineering: Analyzing and Designing Documents for Business Informatics and Web Services.* The MIT Press, 2008.

Weinberger, David. *Everything Is Miscellaneous: The power of the new digital disorder.* Holt Paperbacks, 2007.

Shirky, Clay. *Here Comes Everybody: The Power of Organizing Without Organizations.* The Penguin Press, 2008.

Marco, David. *Building and Managing the Meta Data Repository: A Full Lifecycle Guide.* Wiley Computer Publishing, 2000.

Personalization

Scoble, Robert, and Shel Israel. *Age of Context: Mobile, Sensors, Data and the Future of Privacy.* Patrick Brewster Press, 2014.

Semantic Content

Shuen, Amy. *Web 2.0: A Strategy Guide: Business thinking and strategies behind successful Web 2.0 implementations.* O'Reilly Media, 2008.

Structured Content

Pringle, Alan and Sarah O'Keefe. *The State of Structured Authoring.* Scriptorium Publishing, 2011.

Ament, Kurt. *Single Sourcing: Building Modular Documentation.* William Andrew, 2002.

Glushko, Robert J., and Tim McGrath. *Analyzing and Designing Documents for Business Informatics and Web Services.* The MIT Press, 2005.

Other influential titles

Drucker, Peter F. *Management Challenges for the 21st Century.* HarperBusiness, 2001.

Fayad, Mohamed, and Mauri Laitinen. *Transition to Object-Oriented Software Development.* John Wiley and Sons, 1998.

Sutherland, Jeff. *Scrum: The Art of Doing Twice the Work in Half the Time.* Random House, 2014.

Yagodich, Rick. *Author Experience: Bridging the gap between people and technology in content management.* XML Press, 2014.

Glossary

adaptive content

Content that is designed to adapt to the needs of the customer, not just cosmetically, but also in substance and in capability. Adaptive content automatically responds to the screen size and orientation of any device, but goes further by displaying relevant content that takes advantage of device capabilities such as a GPS or a barometer.

agile

A software and product development approach created with the objective of reducing production time and improving quality. Agile development divides large projects into short, manageable phases, assesses progress frequently, and adapts plans as needed. Agile shares the objectives of lean manufacturing, including reducing waste, increasing productivity, and catching and correcting errors early. Agile methodologies are at the heart of intelligent content.

augmented reality

An enhanced view of a real-world environment, using technology to supplement a normal view with additional content that enhances the experience.

component content management system

A component content management system (CCMS) is a type of content management system designed to manage reusable chunks of semantically rich, structured content at the component level, rather than at the document or file level. A CCMS is required for intelligent content projects.

conditional content

Modular intelligent content designed to vary based on a condition. Conditions enable us to select or exclude content based on the needs of the reader. For example, if the reader is identified as a novice, additional explanatory text could be displayed. Conditions aren't limited to text. They can be applied to almost any type of content.

content

Any text, image, video, decoration, or user-consumable elements that contribute to comprehension.

content analysis

The process and result of conducting a qualitative study of content. It ascertains quality of content against objective quality benchmarks.

content product
An assembly of content components, for example, a press release, an executive profile, a brochure, a course, or a web page.

content reuse
The practice of using content components in multiple content products.

content standard
A design or definition (expressed in a modeling language) considered by an authority as an approved model. Standards include structural and semantic models, processes, and presentation semantics models.

content strategy
The analysis and planning to develop a repeatable system that governs the management of content throughout the entire content lifecycle.

cookie
A small text file sent from a website to a website visitors' web browser and stored in the browser for future reference. Cookies track the movements of website visitors as they navigate a website, remember login credentials and user preferences, and can be customized to perform other functions.

DITA
DITA (Darwin Information Typing Architecture) is an XML data model for authoring and publishing. DITA was originally developed by IBM and in 2005 was approved as an OASIS (Organization for the Advancement of Structured Information Standards) standard. DITA provides supports semantic structure and reuse.

DocBook
An XML standard for creating technical documentation. DocBook is widely used in the open source community and broadly supported by open source tools. This book was produced in DocBook version 5.0. The DocBook standard is maintained by OASIS Open.

document
A purposeful and self-contained content product created to allow organizations and individuals to interact with one another. Documents allow businesses to interact with their prospects, customers, employees, stakeholders, regulators, and others. They are containers that house the information required to conduct business transactions or complete other tasks.

dynamic content

Modular intelligent content that is automatically generated and as-sembled on-demand, using information such as a person's profile, preferences, purchase history, or online behavior. The process that assembles dynamic content can be triggered automatically by events, such as the completion of a business process. Dynamic content is useful for publishing variable content.

See also: variable content

findability

The ease with which relevant content can be located by a consumer.

format free

Format-free content carries no embedded formatting information. This separates formatting from content and makes it easier for content to be prepared automatically for any device.

HTML

HyperText Markup Language (HTML) is the standard markup language used to build web pages. In general, web browsers use HTML files to determine how to display the look-and-feel of content on a website. Web browsers also use HTML files to render web pages in audio format for the visually-impaired or for those who require audio content for safety (while driving, operating equipment) or other reasons. While HTML allows us to add basic semantic descriptors to content (`header`, `footer`, `article`, `section`), it does not provide the flexibility needed to describe intelligent content.

See also: XML

intelligent content

Intelligent content is designed to be modular, structured, reusable, format-free, and semantically rich and, as a consequence, discover-able, reconfigurable, and adaptable.

Internet of Things

The Internet of Things (IoT) refers to the network of connected devices, objects, and people connected together via the internet. The IoT is an ecosystem of technologies equipped with sensors that exchange meaningful data between connected devices, things, and people. Analysts predict the IoT will include over 50 billion connec-ted objects by 2020.

label

In this book, we use the term label to refer to metadata applied to content. For those who are familiar with XML, labels would normally be expressed in XML attributes.

metadata

Attributes of content you can use to structure, semantically define, and target content.

modular content

A form of structured content that is designed, created, and delivered as discrete components within the content whole.

personalization

The practice of targeting content to users based on one or more of the following: who they are; where they are; when, why, and how they access the content; and what device they use to access it.

QR code

A QR (Quick Reference) Code is a machine-readable optical label used to quickly share information about the item to which it is attached. QR codes don't require specialized equipment; most smartphones can understand them. They can be used to provide quick access to almost any type of online information.

re-skin

A slang term used by designers to describe the process of modifying the graphic interface (the skin) of a software application or a website. Re-skinning gives a website or an app a new look-and-feel without necessarily changing functionality.

responsive design

A web development method primarily concerned with creating websites that respond to both user behavior and the screen size and orientation of the device being used to access the site. Responsive websites automatically adjust to provide the best viewing experience possible.

return on investment

Return on investment (ROI) is a measurement that evaluates the anticipated return on an investment compared with the cost of making the investment. If you invest $1,000 and after a year get a return of $1,200, your ROI for that year is 20%. For our purposes, ROI might be measured using the cost of implementing intelligent content as the investment and the combination of cost savings and increased sales as the return.

semantic

Semantically rich content is content to which we've added machine-readable information that describes the content. Semantic information can be conveyed through both structure and metadata.

SGML

Standard Generalized Markup Language (SGML) is a standard for defining markup languages (ISO 8879:1986). Originally designed to make large document sets machine-readable and interoperable, SGML made it possible to describe the structure and other attributes of a document. To better enable the interchange of information over the internet, SGML was re-engineered in 1998 as Extensible Markup Language (XML).

structure

Structured content is predictable content that follows a pattern that humans can read and understand and that computers can process automatically.

tag

In this book, we use the term tag to refer to semantic structural elements. For those who are familiar with XML, tags are equivalent to XML elements.

transclusion

The inclusion of content from one source into another source by hyperlink reference. The presented result appears as though the included content had occurred at the point of reference.

translation

Conversion of content from one language to another.

variable content

Micro-modular intelligent content. Variables are small pieces of content (product name, units of measure, time zones) that vary based on a condition. Conditions enable automated processes to deliver the right content in the right circumstances.

XML

Extensible Markup Language (XML) is an open standard for structured information storage and exchange.

Image Credits

All images licensed from Fotolia.com except for the cover image, the XML Press logo, The Content Wrangler logo, the ICC logo, the images credited to Charles Cooper, and the Plan Ahead T-shirt image.

Chapter 2, *Why Do We Need Intelligent Content?*

- Hands on keyboard image copyright © queidea
- Cost of a click image copyright © nuiiun
- Typewriter image copyright © queidea

Chapter 3, *Why Do Content Marketers Need Intelligent Content?*

- ICC Logo copyright © Content Marketing Institute, used with permission.

Chapter 4, *The Benefits of Intelligent Content*

- Translator image copyright © aeroking

Chapter 5, *Intelligent Content in the Organization*

- Figure 5.1 created by Charles Cooper
- eLearning image copyright © Gstudio Group

Chapter 6, *Opportunity: Increasing Customer Engagement*

- Figure 6.1 created by Charles Cooper

Chapter 7, *Opportunity: Increasing Service Revenue*

- Pete the repair guy image copyright © grafico2011
- MRI image copyright © Andrea Danti

Chapter 8, *Opportunity: Preparing Content for the Future*

- Mac SE image copyright © bramgino
- Smartwatch image copyright © lucadp
- Smart Devices image copyright © Neyro

Chapter 9, *Building Blocks: The Content Perspective*

- Figure 9.1 created by Charles Cooper
- Figure 9.2 created by Charles Cooper
- Figure 9.3 created by Charles Cooper

Chapter 11, *Case Study: Investment Bank*
- Bank case study image copyright © apinan

Chapter 12, *Case Study: Medical Device Company*
- Insulin pump image copyright © Design Praxis

Chapter 13, *Case Study: HMO*
- Guy with heart image copyright © Danomyte
- Figure 13.1 created by Charles Cooper
- Figure 13.2 created by Charles Cooper

Chapter 14, *Possibilities*
- Map image copyright © davooda
- Silhouette image copyright © Pekchar
- Figure 14.1 copyright © mpfphotography
- Adaptive/Responsive Design image created by Charles Cooper

Chapter 16, *Transitioning to Intelligent Content*
- Plan Ahead T-shirt copyright © ComputerGear.org, used with permission.

About Ann Rockley

 Ann Rockley is CEO of The Rockley Group, Inc. Ann has helped Healthcare, Finance, and High Tech companies create structured content strategies and adopt structured content management for more than 25 years. She was instrumental in defining the foundational concepts, strategies, and best practices that have led to the fields of intelligent content, content reuse, and structured content management. Rockley is a frequent contributor to trade and industry publications and a keynote speaker at numerous conferences in North America, Europe, and Asia-Pacific.

Known as the "mother" of content strategy, she introduced the concept with her bestselling book, *Managing Enterprise Content: A Unified Content Strategy*[68]. Ann created the concept of intelligent content and is the founder of the Intelligent Content Conference. Ann has a Master of Information Science from the University of Toronto and is a Fellow of the Society for Technical Communication.

Contact information:

Email:	rockley@rockley.com
Website:	http://www.rockley.com
Twitter:	@arockley
LinkedIn:	http://www.linkedin.com/in/annrockleytrg

About Charles Cooper

 Charles Cooper is VP of The Rockley Group, Inc. He has been involved in creating and testing digital content for more than 20 years. He works with companies to help them understand their content and ensure that it can be intelligently created, managed, and published quickly and consistently – and still meet the needs of their customers. He consults with clients, facilitates modeling sessions, develops taxonomy and workflow strategies, and speaks at conferences worldwide.

Charles is the Rockley Group representative on the OASIS Technical Committee for Augmented Reality.

Contact information:

Email:	cooper@rockley.com
Website:	http://www.rockley.com
Twitter:	@Cooper_42
LinkedIn:	http://www.linkedin.com/in/charlescoopertrg

About Scott Abel

 Known as The Content Wrangler, Scott Abel is an internationally recognized global content strategist who specializes in helping organizations deliver the right content to the right audience, anywhere, anytime, on any device. He writes regularly for business and content industry publications, is frequently selected as a featured presenter at content industry events, and serves on the faculty of the University of California, Berkeley, School of Information.

Scott is a founding member of Content Management Professionals,[1] serves on the Awareness Committee for Translators Without Borders, co-produces several annual conferences: Intelligent Content,[2] Information Development World,[3] and Content Strategy Workshops,[4] and is the producer of The Content Wrangler Content Strategy Series[5] of books from XML Press. The first book in the series, *The Language of Content Strategy*[4], co-produced by Rahel Anne Bailie (with the help of 50 expert contributors), is both a book (print, eBook, audio, and web) and a content marketing case study in single-source, multi-channel publishing.

Scott's message is clear: Content is a business asset worth managing efficiently and effectively. His firm, The Content Wrangler (www.thecontentwrangler.com), exists to help content-heavy organizations adopt the tools, technologies, and techniques they need to connect content to customers.

Contact information:

Email:	scott@thecontentwrangler.com
Website:	http://www.thecontentwrangler.com
Twitter:	@scottabel
LinkedIn:	http://www.linkedin.com/in/scottabel
Facebook:	https://www.facebook.com/scottpatrickabel

---

[1] http://www.cmpros.org/
[2] http://www.intelligentcontentconference.com/
[3] http://www.informationdevelopmentworld.com
[4] http://www.contentstrategyworkshops.com/
[5] http://xmlpress.net/content-strategy/

Index

filtering with, 54
role in discoverability, 2
role in findability, 41
semantically rich, 2, 5, 43–44, 47–48
stylistic, 43
Microsoft Word, 62
mobile devices, publishing content to, 11, 38–39
modular content, 3, 21, 41–42, 52, 54, 76–77
Morgan, Jacob, 71–73
multi-channel display, adapting content for, 71–72

N

New York Times, content publishing experiment by, 19–20

O

online sales, effects of personalized content on, 19

P

page-centric content, 11–12
paper-based publishing, disadvantages of, 7
Pasteur, Louis, 90
personalized content, 18–19, 26, 76
personas, creating for marketing campaigns, 14
Phelps, Andrew, 19–20
Platt, David, 10
print publishing, converting content from print to online, 10–11
process re-engineering, 9
product content, 26
production of content
  authoring, 54–56
  converting from print to online, 10–11
  costs of, 6, 13
  effects of silos on, 15
  efficiency in, 3, 5
  future-proofing, 37–39
  increasing through intelligent content, 19–21
  managing, 51–54
productivity
  detecting bottlenecks in, 10

effects from streamlining and optimizing content marketing, 13
improving for knowledge workers, 8–10
increasing through intelligent content, 19–21
systems designed for, 53
See also costs, work
profiles (user), adapting content to, 71
progressive disclosure, 31
publishing
  automatic, 74
  See also content production
Pulizzi, Joe, 25

Q

questions, asking to analyze and implement intelligent content, 87–88

R

Raia, Mario, 86
re-engineering, process, 9
reconfigurable content, 2
regulated industries, using intelligent content in, 80–81
responsive design, 11, 71–72
reusable content, 3–5, 41, 44–46, 53, 55, 77
revenue (service), increasing with intelligent content, 33–35
risk, reducing with intelligent content, 23–24
Rockley Group, The, 16
Rockley, Ann, 115
  defines intelligent content, 1
  on using technology to produce content, 51–56
  on what makes content intelligent, 41–50
Rugh, John, 15

S

sales, increasing with intelligent content, 18–19, 26
semantically rich content, 5–6, 41, 47–50, 53–54, 56
semantically rich metadata, 2, 5, 43–44, 47–48

Colophon

About the Content Wrangler Content Strategy Book Series

The Content Wrangler Content Strategy Book Series from XML Press provides content professionals with a road map for success. Each volume provides practical advice, best practices, and lessons learned from the most knowledgeable content strategists in the world. Visit the series website for more information xmlpress.net/content-strategy.

About XML Press

XML Press (xmlpress.net) was founded in 2008 to publish content that helps technical communicators be more effective. Our publications support managers, social media practitioners, technical communicators, and content strategists and the engineers who support their efforts.

Our publications are available through most retailers, and discounted pricing is available for volume purchases for educational or promotional use. For more information, send email to orders@xmlpress.net or call us at (970) 231-3624.

The Content Wrangler Content Strategy Book Series

The Language of Content Strategy

Scott Abel and Rahel Anne Bailie

Available Now

Print: $19.95
eBook: $16.95

The Language of Content Strategy is the gateway to a language that describes the world of content strategy. With fifty-two contributors, all known for their depth of knowledge, this set of terms forms the core of an emerging profession and, as a result, helps shape the profession.

Content Audits and Inventories: A Handbook

Paula Ladenburg Land

Available Now

Print: $24.95
eBook: $19.95

Successful content strategy projects start with knowing the quantity, type, and quality of existing assets. Paula Land's new book, *Content Audits and Inventories: A Handbook*, shows you how to begin with an automated inventory, scope and plan an audit, evaluate content against business and user goals, and move forward with actionable insights.

Global Content Strategy: A Primer

Val Swisher

Available Now

Print: $19.95
eBook: $16.95

Nearly every organization must serve its customers around the world. *Global Content Strategy: A Primer* describes how to build a global content strategy that addresses analysis, planning, development, delivery, and consumption of global content that will serve customers wherever they are.

Author Experience: Bridging the gap between people and technology in content management

Rich Yagodich

Available Now

Print: $24.95
eBook: $19.95

Author Experience focuses on the challenges of managing the communication process effectively. It deals with this process from the point of view of those who create and manage content. This book will help you define and implement an author experience that improves quality and efficiency.

Enterprise Content Strategy: A Project Guide

Kevin P. Nichols

Available Now

Print: $24.95
eBook: $19.95

Kevin P. Nichols' *Enterprise Content Strategy: A Project Guide* outlines best practices for conducting and executing content strategy projects. His book is a step-by-step guide to building an enterprise content strategy for your organization.

Intelligent Content: A Primer

Ann Rockley
Charles Cooper
Scott Abel

Available Now

Print: $24.95
eBook: $19.95

Intelligent Content: A Primer introduces the concepts, benefits, and building blocks of intelligent content and gives you the information you need to bring this powerful concept into your organization and begin reaping the benefits.

XMLPress.net

CPSIA information can be obtained
at www.ICGtesting.com
Printed in the USA
FSOW03n1629190216
17122FS

9 781937 434465